# Understanding

# A Training Manual
# for Counsellors and Advocates

DEBORAH SINCLAIR
M.S.W., C.S.W.

The development and publication of this
manual have been funded by the Ontario
Ministry of Community and Social Services,
Family Violence Program.


*Copies of this manual are available from:*

Ontario Government Bookstore
Publications Services Section
880 Bay Street
Toronto, Ontario M7A 1N8
(416) 965-6015
1-800-268-7540
In area code 807: 0-Zenith 67200

ISBN 0-7729-0540-1

# CONTENTS

**APPENDIX A    WHY HUSBAND-BEATING IS A RED HERRING    160**

**APPENDIX B    ASSAULT: DEFINITIONS AND PENALTIES    165**

**APPENDIX C    SEXUAL ASSAULT – THE NEW LAW    167**

**APPENDIX D    THE HISTORICAL CONTEXT    172**

**APPENDIX E    EXAMPLES OF PROTECTIVE ACTIONS    174**

**APPENDIX F    LIST OF USEFUL RESOURCES    175**

**APPENDIX G    RESPONSIBILITIES OF AN ADVOCATE    177**

**EVALUATION    179**

# FOREWORD

I first began working on the issue of wife assault in 1978 as a front-line social worker with the Family Service Association of Metropolitan Toronto. I had the good fortune of being hired by a supportive administrator, Leonard Wengle, who taught me a great deal about the real meaning of social work. I was doubly fortunate to meet two dedicated front-line workers, Doreen Lichtenstein and Susan Harris, who were committed to ending violence in the lives of the women they counselled. Doreen's insights into the needs of wife assault families formed the foundation of a comprehensive project, one of the first of its kind in Canada to deal not only with all members of the family but also to work with the community to effect broader change. Susan's pioneer work in counselling women in a group context became the model for many workers leading support groups for assaulted women across the country. We formed a team known as the Domestic Violence Project (DVP) and although we have since disbanded, the strategies we developed form the basis of the material in this manual. Our primary focus was in helping assaulted women find ways to protect themselves from further violence.

Since that time, I have worked with well over seven hundred women. At first, we did not have contact with their husbands, nor did we spend time encouraging their children to talk. As our understanding deepened, we recognized that many women did **not** want their marriages to end, but rather wanted an end to the violence. At their request, we began to invite their husbands into our offices to speak with us. If women were going to remain in their homes or return to their husbands, we felt it was our responsibility to work with their husbands as well.

So began our involvement with men who assault their wives. David Currie, our co-worker, was invited to join the team in 1979 because we believed it was important for men as well as women to take an active role in solving this problem. David's insights into what would help assaultive men change formed the foundation for men's programming in Ontario and much of Canada.

Our involvement with the children of these families also began at the request of the women. As mothers began to feel better about themselves, they were better able to focus their energies on their children. They knew their children were suffering. We panicked. Our counselling experience was with adults, not children. We searched the literature but little material was available. We realized that to understand their needs we would have to do exactly the same as we had done with their mothers and their fathers. We began to talk to the children. More importantly, we started to listen.

The counselling approach suggested in this manual evolved from these beginnings. We use this approach because it works; men stop being violent, women stop being victims of assault, and children learn that violence is not acceptable. These conclusions have been confirmed by my own observations. Over the years we have witnessed clients making dramatic behavioural and attitudinal changes in relatively short periods of time. We have leaned heavily on their opinions of what helped them and what hindered them. When in doubt, we turned to them for answers. Inevitably they proved to be our greatest teachers.

As our work evolved, we realized that counselling was **not** enough. If wife assault truly was a social problem, it would require social solutions. To address this need, we developed and implemented various aspects of a community model aimed at improving services for assaulted women and their families. As part of that model, I helped found the Emily Stowe Shelter for Women in the community where I worked -- Scarborough, Ontario.

Our team was committed to sharing all that we had learned with other counsellors and advocates. Professional development became an integral part of our work. During the past seven years, I have conducted over one hundred training sessions, meeting more than two thousand workers in the process. This manual is written in response to many of the questions raised in those sessions.

## ACKNOWLEDGEMENTS

Many people made this manual possible.  I would like to thank the following for their valuable contributions:

o     The women in the shelter movement who form my support system, challenge my ideas and reaffirm my values.  They have been my richest resource.  Like assaulted women, they struggle for daily survival against great odds.  They seldom have the time, energy or money to document their experiences and to put their knowledge onto paper.  Too often, others receive credit that should rightly be theirs.

o     The members of Education Wife Assault, who volunteer their time and expertise to expand our knowledge and broaden our understanding of the pertinent issues.  I have relied heavily on their resources.

o     The women, men and children, who courageously shared their stories. They taught me what was important and what they needed to end the violence in their lives.

o     Shirley Endicott Small deserves a most special mention.  I looked forward to our weekly meetings, confident that her challenging comments would stimulate my thinking, sharpen my focus and enable me to translate my experience into written word.  Her enthusiastic willingness to assist me in this project was done without remuneration and reflects her commitment to ending violence in the lives of women.

o     Marg Kimmerer, who typed the manuscript under far-from-perfect conditions and never failed to provide helpful feedback and constant encouragement.

o     Betty Notar, Mary Parthun, Carol Holmes, Barbara Pressman, Jenny Roberts, Carolyn Skelly, Fran Pendrith and Diane Isaac, who read all or parts of the first draft and whose comments brought greater clarity to the final product. Diane Isaac deserves special mention for co-ordinating the writing and production of the manual from beginning to end with infinite patience and a sense of humour.  Her administrative skill saved the day on more that one occasion.

o     Daphne Hart, whose creative ability and sensitivity to the issue of violence against women and children are reflected in the imaginative design of the manual.

o     Greg Ioannou, who made the tedious task of editing the manual a pleasant experience.  He even delayed picking up his new kittens, Chess and Checkers, until we finished the very final pages.

o     Susan Harris, who in the midst of her own demanding work in Winnipeg not only volunteered her time to write the chapter on support groups for assaulted women, but also in our phone conversations gave me insights into counselling issues that no one else could.  Had we anticipated the exorbitant phone bills coming our way, we might have chosen to meet in person.  Surely air fare would have been less costly.

o     Maureen Adams, who was always available to give me constructive feedback and continuous support.  The beautiful spring flowers she sent with a note of encouragement sustained me at a crucial point in the writing process.

o     My husband, David Currie, whose support for me and faith in this project kept me going.  He willingly read all of the material from the beginning draft to the final stages, offering valuable suggestions throughout.  In the midst of a demanding time for himself, he not only undertook to write the chapter on group work for men but also willingly took over more than his share of household and child-care duties.  He tolerated my long absences, locked away in the study, with patience and a sense of humour, always ready to remind me of the importance of this work when I lost sight of the goal.  His ability to put into practice the principles he believes in continually reaffirms my belief that men and women can have equal, loving relationships based on mutual respect.

o     My daughter, Meg, whose sunny smile brightened many a day and continually reminded me of the importance of balancing work with play.  Not only did she share me with the writing of this manual but also even withstood interrupted nursings as I rushed to capture some elusive idea on paper.  Her resilient, trusting nature reaffirms my belief in children's strength and renews my commitment to work towards creating a non-violent world for her to grow up in.

## CORNERSTONE PRINCIPLES

The principles upon which this manual is based are:

1.    Violence has no place in the family.

2.    The community has a right and a responsibility to get involved.

3.    Wife assault is **not** the result of an argument that gets out of hand.
It goes much beyond the normal marital tension that all couples experience.

4.    A comprehensive community approach is essential.  Counselling is **not** enough.

5.    Once violence has started, it will **not** stop spontaneously.  Active intervention is needed from the community, especially from the justice system.

6.    Prevention means addressing the social roots of wife assault, **not** just the symptoms.  Education is a prerequisite to prevention.

## PART ONE   BACKGROUND

> The counsellor excuses herself from the interview.
> Outside her office door, she fights to regain her
> composure. How could my client go back? He's a
> monster. He'll kill her next time! I'm so frustrated,
> angry, scared. What did I do wrong? Maybe, I pushed
> her too quickly to leave him, to get out. Now it's
> backfired. I feel so damned helpless . . . .

Countless workers have shared these feelings with me. Wife assault is not an easy subject to deal with. It hurts. It is scary. We were seldom trained to think about it, let alone counsel real, live victims. Some of us hide behind our professional masks, desperately trying to sound knowledgeable and to make sense of it, but inside we tremble. It makes us sick and we feel inadequate, embarrassed, frustrated. Many times we become part of the problem. Thinking back over my years of working with assaulted women and their families, the following examples come to mind:

o      the **police officer** who could not take the assault seriously because "tomorrow she would just go back for more."

o      the **minister** who believed so strongly in the sanctity of the family that he failed to see the dangerous reality of his parishioner's home life.

o      the **social worker** who unwittingly increased the risk for her client's safety by encouraging the couple to air their differences in each other's presence.

o      the **shelter worker** who felt like a personal failure when one of the residents she was attached to, returned to her husband's promises of "never, no more."

o      the **counsellor** who held the victim responsible for the continuation of the violence: "She could fight back or just leave, couldn't she?"

o      the **doctor** who prescribed Valium because he felt helpless to do anything else.

o      the **lawyer** who pulled her hair out in frustration when, after she initiated all the paper work for a divorce, the woman changed her mind.

o      the **Justice of the Peace** who, when confronted with a woman's request to lay assault charges, handed her a letter urging her to seek marital counselling with her husband. "She doesn't want to send her husband to jail, does she?"

o      the **Children's Aid Society worker,** who in concern for the children, increased their risk, and their mother's risk, by prematurely entering the home unequipped to deal with their safety and protection.

o       the **Public Health Nurse** who endangered herself by confronting the violent husband on his home turf.

o       the **hospital-based counsellor** who insisted on joint counselling immediately, even when the wife was in obvious need of medical attention.

This manual seeks to demystify the violence, to explain the facts, to dispel the myths and, most importantly, to equip workers to intervene effectively in families that are torn apart by violence. It is written for anyone who is committed to ending violence in our homes. Professional credentials are of less importance than your level of awareness, desire to learn, sensitivity and common sense. Regardless of our educational background, most of us did not learn about violence in our formal training, at least in any meaningful way. Therefore, whether we come from a professional discipline, a paraprofessional discipline or are dedicated volunteers, we are all in the same boat. How do we intervene in a way that maintains each person's integrity while ensuring the safety and protection of all family members?

This manual will be most meaningful to counsellors and advocates who will have ongoing contact with families. However, those sections that deal with increasing general awareness will be helpful to anyone -- legal worker, judge or neighbour -- having contact with violence in a family. In this manual, I use the terms "advocate" and "counsellor" interchangeably. Every counsellor must be prepared to act as an advocate, although every advocate does not have to be a trained counsellor. I particularly like the term "advocate" because it describes someone who believes, defends and supports victims of wife assault and champions the ending of violence against women. It also implies that the vast majority of assaulted women and violent men are not mentally or emotionally ill and do not require the traditional forms of professional intervention.

It is important not to use portions of the manual in isolation but rather to use it in its entirety as a means to develop a comprehensive understanding of the issue. However if you do not have the time to read the manual from cover to cover, skip to those parts most useful for your immediate work. Then come back at a later date and read it at your leisure. An overall familiarity with the material will enhance your intervention, even if you are only working with one aspect of the problem. If you are able to develop empathy for each member of the family, you can't help but find this work much less stressful. Realistic expectations are also much easier to adhere to if you have a clear and comprehensive understanding of the entire issue.

The special problems of minority women -- native women, immigrant women, handicapped women -- have not been addressed in this manual. I believe the basic principles suggested apply to all women's lives regardless of background. However, counsellors and advocates have a responsibility to sensitize themselves to the unique situations of specific groups of women whenever possible.*

I have assumed that counsellors reading this manual have a basic level of therapeutic skill. The signs of an effective counsellor are recognizing your limits of expertise and knowing what to do when you meet them. This manual will assist the counsellor to find those limits and possibly go beyond them.

The manual does not pretend to have all the answers. It is best used as an adjunct to the training sessions given by myself and others in the field. Reading a book or working by yourself can be lonely and isolating experiences, so we need a forum to exchange ideas with others who are also struggling against violence.

---

* Refer to Monica Ruitort and Shirley Endicott Small, Working with Assaulted Immigrant Women: A Handbook For Lay Counsellors. Toronto: Education Wife Assault, 1984.

# 1. INTRODUCTION TO WIFE ASSAULT

Violence in the home is a complex issue. It provokes intense emotional reactions, ranging from disbelief and horror to outright rage and even a desire to physically retaliate. It touches each of us deeply when we allow it to penetrate our defences.

Why is this subject so difficult that we resist talking about it or even reading about it? Perhaps it stems from our strong desire to believe in the goodness and security of the family and that our home is our haven, a safe place where we can let down our hair, take off our masks and be ourselves. A place where we will be loved and accepted unconditionally. A place where we can grow and learn about ourselves and others. Does this place exist? Perhaps for some the family is a liberating experience. But for many **the home is a prison.**

In fact, for too many women the streets are safer than their own homes. Violence against women in the home is often hidden behind such terms as spouse abuse, marital violence, couple battering, domestic violence and inter-spousal abuse. These terms cloud the issue, mislead the reader, obscure the facts. They imply that each marital partner is equally likely to play the role of offender or victim in violent incidents, that the frequency and the severity used by each is similar and that the social-historical meaning and the consequences of these acts are the same. This is **not** the case!

The majority of violence in the home is directed at women and children.

o    Dobash and Dobash, two Scottish researchers, found that **75.8%** of all violence in the home is actually assault against the wife.[1]

o    Dr. Jack Byles in a study of calls for help to the Hamilton police in 1974 showed women to be the victims in **95%** of the calls.[2]

o    Dr. Pat Kincaid in a study in Toronto of family court records reflected the same figure, 95% of the assaults were against the wife.[3]

---

[1]    Dobash, Rebecca Emerson, and Russell Dobash. <u>Violence Against Wives.</u> New York: Free Press, 1979.

[2]    Byles, Jack. "Family Violence in Hamilton." <u>Canadian Mental Health.</u> 28:1, 1980.

[3]    Kincaid, Pat. <u>The Omitted Reality: Husband Wife Violence in Ontario and Policy Implications for Education.</u> Toronto: Learnsx Press, 1982.

My own clinical practice and that of my colleagues reflect a very similar statistical breakdown. Although there is already a great deal of excellent material on child abuse, there is still little practical material available on wife assault.

It is also my belief that eliminating wife abuse would substantially reduce the occurrence of child abuse. Efforts to enhance mothers' safety will, in most cases, indirectly ensure children's safety. For these reasons, this manual will be limited to those violent acts committed against women in the role of wife. This is not intended to undermine the significance or the seriousness of violence directed at other members of the family.

**All Violence Is Unacceptable!**

For counsellors who encounter other victims, the basic principles outlined in this manual can be applied regardless of the victim's position in the family.*

### Definition of Wife Assault

Wife assault involves the intent by the husband to intimidate, either by threat or by use of physical force on the wife's person or property. The purpose of the assault is to control her behaviour by the inducement of fear. Underlying all abuse is a power imbalance between the victim and the offender.**

### Forms of Wife Assault[4]

**Physical** assault is the most obvious form to identify. It includes slapping, punching, kicking, shoving, choking and pinching. Other types of physical assault include throwing things (such as acid) into the victim's face, inflicting

---

\*  In most training sessions someone asks "What about battered husbands?" For this reason, I have included a paper in the Appendix written by Shirley Endicott Small addressing this issue. See Appendix A.

\*\*  This definition is used for the purpose of intervention only. The legal definition is found in Appendix B. You have probably noticed by now that I do not use the term "batter." This is for two reasons: the term is derived from the American judicial system and is consistent with their Criminal Code, which is not the case in Canada. Secondly, the term "batter" often conjures up serious injuries requiring hospitalization. Offenders and victims often cannot identify with this if their situation does not appear as severe. "My husband doesn't batter me. He only hits me." As one former client said recently at a public forum in reaction to this word, "Fish and bread are battered, women are assaulted."

[4]  Ganley, Anne. Court-Mandated Counselling For Men Who Batter: A Three Day Workshop For Mental Health Professionals. Washington: Center for Women Policy Studies, 1982.

cigarette burns on the body, using objects such as a vacuum cleaner hose, a coat hanger or a belt with a buckle to beat the victim. The use of weapons such as guns, knives or axes may result in the ultimate act of violence, murder. The abuse is directed towards the body, sometimes to parts of the body that do not bruise easily, such as pubic bone, skull or the bottoms of the feet.

Counsellors and clients sometimes view the assault on a continuum from mild (slap or push) to severe (use of weapons) assaults. This can be misleading and dangerous if the intent is to minimize certain kinds of assaults and view them as less worthy of attention and intervention. However, it is a logical framework to use if the intent is to assess the severity by examining the consequences. A "small shove" may be a push down the stairs resulting in a damaged spine. A slap with an open hand may result in a broken nose. To accurately assess the immediate danger would mean not only an examination of the actual violence but also the consequences of the assault. Even when the assault does not result in visible damage, it still should be taken seriously as it may be the beginning of a pattern that will increase in frequency and severity over time. It can end in murder.

**Sexual** assault* often starts with demeaning women through jokes, name-calling and unwanted touching. It includes any forced sexual activities, as well as excessive jealousy and sexual accusations. Some victims describe being forced to engage in sexual acts that they find distasteful or painful, such as group sex, anal penetration or penetrating objects in sex. The victim's sexual needs are seldom attended to. Sex is sometimes used as a punishment by rejection of her as a sexual partner. The husband often flaunts stories of his extramarital affairs and subjects his wife to unfavourable comparisons with other women. Women describe the humiliation of being forced to tolerate, and engage in, sexual practices portrayed in violent pornographic magazines bought by their husbands and openly displayed in their family home. Sometimes, the victim will not even think that she has been sexually abused. One common situation involves the woman who submits to her husband's sexual demands because she does not feel she has the freedom to refuse without serious repercussions. She feels she cannot say "no" because submission is viewed as part of her wifely duty. Sexual assault is often accompanied by threats of violence or actual violence. It can end in murder.

---

\*      As of January, 1983, in Canada it is against the law for a man to sexually assault his wife. See Appendix C.

**Psychological** abuse differs from emotional or verbal abuse. It has greater power to induce fear in the victim because the threats of violence have been accompanied by at least one incident of physical abuse. The offender has demonstrated his ability to carry out his threats. Psychological abuse can take various forms:

1.  making threats, such as suicidal threats, violent threats against the victim and her loved ones, threats to harm her property and pets, threats to kidnap the children, threats of deportation if she is under his sponsorship, threats to use information he may have about her past life against her if she leaves him.

2.  forcing her to do degrading things, such as cutting up her favourite dress, washing her mouth out with soap, licking the dishes clean.

3.  doing things that will terrorize her, such as driving through red lights, speeding on slippery streets, tying a noose around her neck, playing with a gun or knife in her presence.

4.  verbally attacking her personality, attitudes or beliefs or belittling any efforts she makes to better herself.

5.  controlling her activities, disrupting her routines, depriving her of necessary needs (such as sleep, food, sex, money) isolating her from family and friends.

These kinds of psychological tortures are designed to wear the victim down. She is in constant fear for her safety. Her situation is extremely unpredictable as she seldom knows **if** he will physically harm her. Its insidious nature debilitates her capacity to think clearly, thus creating a life-threatening atmosphere. It can end in murder.

**Destruction of Property** is less likely to be taken seriously by everyone involved. Because he appears to direct his rage at objects, he is perceived as less threatening by outsiders. "At least, he didn't harm her. . . ." This is not the case. On closer examination, you will find that he is very deliberate in choosing his targets. He destroys **her** property; her photo albums, her cherished mementos, her favourite dress. His message is clear: "Stay in line, because the next time it could be you. . . ." When women share with you their worry about not wanting to leave their home out of fear their valuables will be destroyed - believe them. Unless they are in immediate danger, it is more effective to help them develop a plan of action that will protect not only them but also their personal property. Pets are not immune to his destruction, nor are children. Both can be used as a means to intimidate and control her behaviour. It can end in murder.

## The Extent of the Problem

Wife assault is a silent crime, a hidden crime. By far the majority of assaults go unreported. Usually, they occur in the privacy of a home. Seldom are there witnesses. Even when brought to the attention of authorities, incidents of wife assault are seldom documented and even less likely to be consistently collected as important data in the social service network. Last spring, in preparation for the training phase of a Ministry of Community and Social Services project, I informally surveyed six of the major social service agencies in Metropolitan Toronto to ascertain the documentation kept regarding the incidence of wife assault in their caseloads. Only two agencies contacted kept track of this information.

For any social problem to be taken seriously, it needs to be proven that it affects a significant proportion of the population. Even though we may never know the true incidence of wife assault in the general population, it is imperative that we take every opportunity to clearly document it when we have access to the information. The following statistics have proven useful for stressing the extent of the problem. Wherever possible, local statistics should be added to this list, as they carry the greatest weight in raising public awareness.

o    One in 10 Canadian women are victims of wife assault (thought to be a very conservative estimate by many of the experts working in this area).[5]

o    The FBI estimates a woman is severely beaten in the U.S. every 18 seconds.

o    Violence against wives will occur at least once during two-thirds of all marriages.[6]

o    25% of all wives are severely beaten during the course of their marriage.[7]

o    One in five families requesting counselling were identified as wife assault victims at first contact. This figure increases as workers gain greater expertise.[8]

---

[5]    MacLeod, Linda. Wife Battering in Canada: The Vicious Circle. Ottawa: Canadian Advisory Council on the Status of Women, 1980.

[6]    Roy, Maria (ed.). The Abusive Partner: An Analysis of Domestic Battering. New York: Van Nostrand Reinhold, 1980.

[7]    Strauss, Murray, et al. Behind Closed Doors: Violence in the American Family. New York: Anchor Press, 1980.

[8]    Harris, Susan, and Deborah Sinclair. Domestic Violence Project: A Comprehensive Model For Intervention into the Issue of Domestic Violence. Toronto: Family Services Association of Metropolitan Toronto, July, 1981.

o    Two-fifths of all homicides in Canada are between spouses. The vast majority of the victims are women. Those women who do kill their spouses are usually acting in self-defense.[9]

**Facts About Wife Assault**

**1.    Wife assault is a crime.**

It is punishable by law. (See Appendix B for Definitions and Penalties outlined in the Criminal Code.)

**2.    Women are most vulnerable to being assaulted in their intimate relationships.***

These relationships include legal and commonlaw marriages, dating relationships and even when a couple is no longer living together, although it occurs most frequently among married couples. One researcher goes so far as to call the marriage license a hitting license.[10]

**3.    Wife assault is rarely an isolated incident.**

One study demonstrated women being beaten as many as 35 times prior to their contact with the police at the time of the study.[11]

**4.    Wife assault increases in severity over time.**

Although no formal studies have been made, my clinical experience and that of my colleagues suggests that without direct intervention, assaults usually become more severe over time.

**5.    Wife assault causes serious and sometimes even permanent damage.**

Twenty percent of visits to emergency medical services are the direct result of wife assault.[12]

**6.    Victims of assault are vulnerable to self-destructive behaviour.**

---

*    For the purpose of this manual, the terms "husband" and "wife" are used interchangeably with the term "partner." These terms reflect an intimate relationship between a man and a woman, whether the couple is married or unmarried.

[9]    Statistics Canada, Justice Statistics Division. Homicide in Canada: A Statistical Synopsis. Ottawa: 1982.

[10]    Strauss, Murray, ibid.

[11]    Jaffe, Peter, and Carole Anne Burris. An Integrated Response to Wife Assault: A Community Approach Model. Ottawa: the Solicitor General of Canada, July, 1982.

[12]    Stark, Even, and A. Filitcraft. "Medical therapy as Repression: The Case of the Battered Woman." Health and Medicine. Summer/Fall, 1982.

One study suggests that wife assault accounts for 25% of all suicide attempts. The same study concludes that assaulted women are far more likely to attempt suicide than non-assaulted women and do so repeatedly.[13]

## 7.     Wife assault is not a recent phenomenon.

Recent publicity may lead you to think it is on the rise, but in fact it's always been a hidden part of our community. Women, angry and tired of being victimized, are demanding that it become a public issue, a social problem in need of remedy. Credit for breaking the silence must go to the pioneers in the battered women's movement. By providing safety through shelters, assaulted women came forward and were believed.

## 8.     Wife assault has been condoned throughout history.*

It is only within the last 100 years that wife assault has been considered illegal. Prior to that time, laws regulated the **extent** to which men could physically discipline their wives. One example is the popular "Rule of Thumb" termed by the English codifier of common law, William M. Blackstone, in 1767.[14] This law permitted husbands to enforce domestic discipline in their homes as long as they used a switch or stick no broader than the width of their thumb. It was applied not only to wives but also to children and apprentices. All members of his household were seen as his property to do with as he saw fit if within reason. In Canada, it wasn't until 1968 with the Federal Divorce Act that cruelty became grounds for divorce. A woman, prior to 1968, would have to have visible proof of severe physical/mental abuse endangering her life before she could claim for alimony. In the words of one Ontario Chief Justice

> a husband may subject his wife, daily and even hourly to
> such treatment as makes her life a veritable hell on
> earth and she is without remedy if she is robust enough
> to suffer it all without impairment of her physical
> health or her mentality.[15]

## Myths About Wife Assault

Many of us are victim to commonly held beliefs about wife assault. These beliefs lead to an inappropriate analysis of the problem, which results in ineffective interventions that fail to stop violent behaviour. Workers often express frustration and helplessness at this stage and, to cope with feelings of inadequacy, the victim gets blamed and the offender gets excused. This

---

*      See Appendix D for a sample speech on the historical context of wife assault written by Shirley Endicott Small.

[13]      Marriage and Divorce Today: The Professional Newsletter for Family Therapy Practitioners. 10, No. 9, October, 1984.

[14]      Langley, Roger, and Richard Levy. Wife Beating: The Silent Crisis. New York: Pocket Books, 1979.

[15]      Dranoff, Linda. Women in Canadian Law. Toronto: Fitzhenry and Whiteside, 1977.

phenomenon of victim-blaming and excusing the offender perpetuates a belief in the myths. The cycle is then complete, as shown in Figure 1.

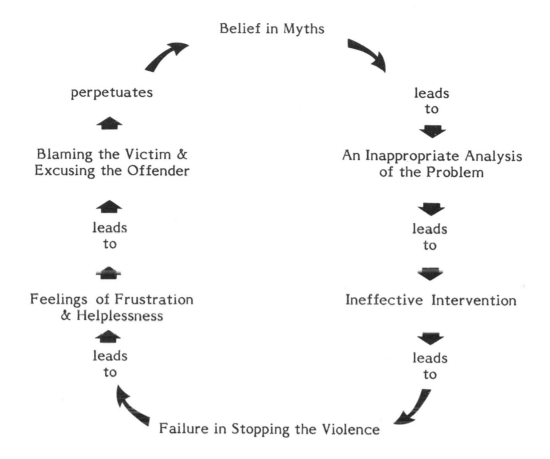

Belief in Myths

perpetuates

Blaming the Victim &
Excusing the Offender

leads
to

Feelings of Frustration
& Helplessness

leads
to

Failure in Stopping the Violence

leads
to

An Inappropriate Analysis
of the Problem

leads
to

Ineffective Intervention

leads
to

These myths are also often believed by the families we see. Thus, our clients are as vulnerable to entrapment in this cycle as we are. We must first sensitize ourselves to the realities of violence as a necessary prerequisite to effective intervention. Some of the most common myths include:

MYTH:    **Men who assault their wives are mentally ill.**

REALITY:    Wife assault is too widespread to be explained away by mental illness. Most men who assault their wives confine their violence to the privacy of their own home. The abuse is often directed to particular parts of the body that will not visibly bruise; obvious restraint and forethought is necessary to accomplish this. Violent husbands are not likely to attack their bosses when frustrated. If the man was truly mentally ill, he would lack the ability to be selective in his targets and controlled in his administration of abuse.

MYTH:    **Alcohol causes a man to beat his wife.**

REALITY:    While alcohol is often abused by the violent partner, it is not the cause of the violence. Rather, it facilitates the use of physical force by allowing the offender to abdicate responsibility for his behaviour. Some men become intoxicated in order to act out their violent wishes.

MYTH:  **Only poor women get beaten.**

REALTY:  Victims of wife assault come from all walks of life -- rich/poor, black/white, rural/urban, educated/uneducated, full-time housewives/career women. There are no exceptions. However, violence in the upper classes is more likely to be hidden from public scrutiny because these women may have more to lose by exposing their situation.

MYTH:  **Women provoke violence. Therefore, they deserve what they get.**

REALITY:  No woman ever deserves to be beaten, regardless of the kind of person she is. Provocation is an excuse the offender uses to avoid responsibility for his own behaviour. Many people support his view by also examining the victim's behaviour or personality for clues as to the cause of the assault. Excuse-making perpetuates the use of violence as an acceptable method of problem-solving and leads the offender to believe he is justified in using force to get his own way.

MYTH:  **Women enjoy the abuse and find it sexually stimulating.**

REALITY:  Women do not find pleasure in abuse, nor is it a sexual turn-on. In fact, women are terrified, horrified and disgusted when their partners turn on them. The "masochist" label (someone who derives pleasure from pain or seeks it out) is often used in an irresponsible manner by uninformed people to explain the assaulted women's dilemma. Although women often return to an abusive partner, it is not the violence they are returning to but the hope that it has stopped. Applying this label to assaulted women is demeaning and disrespectful and is one more way to blame the victim.

MYTH:  **If women were really bothered by the assault, they would speak up.**

REALITY:  Assault victims remain silent for valid reasons. They believe they and their loved ones will be at even greater risk if they disclose the abuse. They may believe the abuse is their fault so feel great shame and embarrassment. Female role conditioning, with its emphasis on passivity and compliance, perpetuates a victim position in life. Ironically, those women courageous enough to challenge the silence are often not listened to or believed anyway.

MYTH:  **Men who beat their wives are a danger to the community.**

REALITY:  Wife-beaters seldom attack anyone outside their family. They know they would not likely get away with it. They reserve their rage for their wives, realizing that the consequences will be minor. Perhaps if these men were a greater danger to the community at large, major deterrents would already be in place.

MYTH:  **Assaulted women could leave their abusive partners if they wanted to.**

REALITY:  Women remain in abusive relationships for many reasons. Some are committed to their marriages and desperately want them to be successful. They hope he will change. For others, leaving is not an option because they have no place to go nor money to live on. Poverty is a very real possibility for assaulted women, especially those with children. Fear of being further harmed keeps them imprisoned in a violent relationship. Women often describe their husbands' threats to kill them if they leave.

MYTH: **Pregnant women are protected from violent attacks.**

REALITY: In fact, women who are pregnant are **more** vulnerable to violence. Many women describe the abuse starting when they were first pregnant or the violence became more severe during a pregnancy. Pregnant women have even less access to resources and thus are more dependent on their partners than at non-pregnant times. Husbands take advantage of this dependent phase knowing that their wives will be less able to counter their attacks.

## Suggested Reading - General Overview

Dobash, Russell, P., and Dobash, Rebecca Emerson. Violence Against Wives. New York: Free Press, 1979.

Harris, Susan, and Sinclair, Deborah. Domestic Violence Project: A Comprehensive Model Into the Issue of Domestic Violence. Toronto: Family Service Association of Metropolitan Toronto, 1981.

Hilberman, Elaine, and Munson, Kit. Sixty Battered Women. Victimology 2 (3-4) 1977-1978. pp. 460-470.

Jaffe, Peter, and Burris, Carole Anne. An Integrated Response to Wife Assault: A Community Model. Ottawa: The Solicitor General of Canada, July, 1982.

Kincaid, Pat. The Omitted Reality: Husband - Wife Violence in Ontario and Policy Implications for Education. Toronto: Learnxs Press, 1982.

MacLeod, Linda. Wife Battering In Canada: The Vicious Circle. Ottawa: Canadian Advisory Council on the Status of Women.

Martin, Del. Battered Wives. New York: Pocket Books, 1977.

Pressman, Barbara. Family Violence: Origins and Treatment. Guelph, Ontario: University of Guelph, 1984.

Schecter, Susan. Women and Male Violence. Boston: South End Press, 1982.

Small, Shirley Endicott. Wife Assault An Overview of the Problem in Canada. Toronto: Education Wife Assault, 1980.

Waldman, Gerry. Law Concerning Domestic Violence. Toronto: Education Wife Assault, May, 1982.

## 2 WHY WOMEN REMAIN IN VIOLENT RELATIONSHIPS

We know that any woman is vulnerable to being a victim of violence, but there is no way of predicting which women will be victims. Why does one woman take immediate protective action after a single assault while another woman will suffer repeated assaults? As counsellors we seldom see the woman who is assaulted once. We have no estimates of how many women this happens to. They are unlikely to come to us for assistance. We do see, however, the woman who is assaulted repeatedly. What happens to this woman **before** the assault occurs that makes it difficult for her to take protective action? What happens **after** the assault to keep her in a victim position? We know from experience that these questions must be answered before effective service can be given.

The counsellor's task is to evaluate with the woman those factors that are most pressing in her not changing her situation. Figure 2 has been helpful in delineating some of the issues that contribute to the assaulted woman's situation.[1]

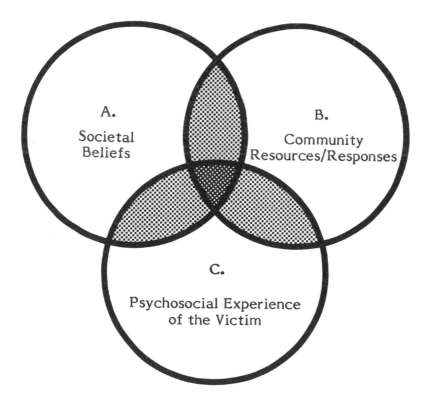

A.
Societal
Beliefs

B.
Community
Resources/Responses

C.

Psychosocial Experience
of the Victim

---

[1] Conroy, Kathryn. "Long-term Treatment Issues with Battered Women," in S. Flanza (ed.) The Many Faces of Family Violence. Springfield, Illinois: Charles C. Thomas: 1982. pp. 24-33.

**Circle A** represents the societal beliefs that contribute to keeping a woman trapped in an abusive relationship.

**Circle B** represents both the responses she receives from her community and her access to resources that will enable her to leave an abusive relationship.

**Circle C** represents the psychological experience of the assaulted woman that contributes to her victimization.

The counsellor must have a comprehensive understanding of the interplay between all those factors that complicate the lives of assaulted women. Most assaulted women tend to fall within the shaded areas in the figure. Experienced workers have reached a consensus on the factors that contribute to her situation. This section discusses those factors.

### Societal Beliefs Contribute to Violence Against Wives

All of us have been brought up with, certain values and beliefs about being men and women, about marriage and divorce, about privacy of the home and about the expression of affection and anger. Some of the values and beliefs embedded in our society complicate the lives of assaulted women.

#### The Traditional Female Role

A woman is taught from an early age to passively accept what life brings her. She often goes from her father's home to her husband's home. She gives up her father's name to take on her husband's name. She is socialized to believe that her worth as a person will be measured by her ability to "catch a man" and to "keep him." She grows up believing she will be taken care of economically and socially by a man in exchange for caring for his home and children. If she pursues a career, it will be secondary to her husband's. She is expected to assume a dependent, helpless, child-like stance in the world, while the men in her life make decisions affecting her future. Her pleasure is expected to come from pleasing others, especially men. She seeks approval as the means to validate her self. Some of the common statements that contribute to her remaining in an abusive relationship and reflect the stereotypic expectations of women are:

> "You made your bed, now lie in it."

> "Marriage is not a bed of roses. You have to take the good with the bad."

> "It's your duty to stand by him. He must be under stress."

Training for the traditional female role prepares a woman well for the position of victim. She has been trained to think herself selfish if she puts her needs ahead of others. In an abusive relationship, she runs the risk of being called a martyr or a masochist when she loyally defends her partner, when she is merely fulfilling the role she has been trained for. She is placed under tremendous pressure to make the marriage work, or at least **appear** to make it work. She is held responsible for the success or failure of the union. For the assaulted woman, this places her in a Catch-22 position. If she protects herself from the violence by leaving, she may be accused of desertion. If she remains in the abusive relationship, she is accused of needing the abuse, or worse, deriving pleasure from it. Enormous conflict is created for the assaulted woman, since to fail to hold her marriage together means to fail in her most basic role expectation.

## The Privacy of the Home

Our society teaches that the family is a sacred place. No one from the outside has a right to intervene. Family loyalty is expected. What goes on behind closed doors is private business.

"Don't air your dirty laundry in public."

"This is my home, I can do what I want here."

"It's not my business to interfere in private family
matters."

This belief keeps neighbours, concerned family and friends, and even professionals from effectively intervening when they witness or hear of the abuse. While there is some merit to "privacy of the home" it is often used as an excuse for irresponsibility and inactivity. It encourages women to struggle and suffer in silence.

## The Two-Parent Family as the Ideal

Because the two-parent family is considered the ideal, many people feel that the family should stay together at all costs. A higher value is placed on the preservation of the traditional family unit than on the safety and happiness of the individual family members. As well, there is a belief that children need their father present in the home, regardless of the quality of the relationship or the risks they encounter as a result of his presence.

"She should stay for the sake of the family."

"A woman's place is in the home."

"He's a good father even if he does hit her
once in awhile."

This kind of thinking keeps families together for all the wrong reasons. Children are not safe in a home where there is continued abuse. They do not need a father who models violent behaviour as a way to solve problems. They do not benefit from a mother who models passive, victim-like behaviour. Children are our future resources and deserve the best possible start. Pressuring assaulted mothers to keep the family intact not only endangers her safety but also erodes her ability to provide quality care to the children.

## Victim-Blaming

Blaming the victim is so pervasive that it demands special attention. Common statements that reflect this belief include:

"What did you do to make him hit you?"

"Your husband's such a nice guy. You must have done something wrong."

"If you hadn't married him, then you wouldn't be in this spot."

Such statements feed into the assaulted woman's negative self-image. They heighten her self-doubt and convince her that she may really be responsible for his violence. This is one of the easiest pitfalls for the worker to fall into, especially if efforts to assist her have not been successful and the worker is feeling frustrated and angry. Women are not angels. Some you may find particularly unlikeable. It is tempting to hold them responsible for at least part of the abuse. However, the bottom line must be no woman ever deserves to be beaten, regardless of the kind of person she is.

## Shortage of Resources and Community Attitudes
## Perpetuate Violence Against Wives

It is important for the worker to have a clear understanding of the reality the assaulted woman faces when she reaches out for help for two reasons:

1.    so you don't fall into the trap of blaming her when she cannot make changes as rapidly as you think she should.

2.    so you can prepare **her** not to blame herself when she confronts obstacles that slow her progress.

Most service providers are painfully aware of the economic realities facing their clients. They include conditions such as:

## Housing

o     a lack of emergency shelter beds.

o     little access to second-stage housing (a must for women and children in transition).

o     little access to affordable, permanent housing.

## Employment

o     little access to jobs, particularly ones with decent wages.

o     too few retraining programs for women forced to enter the job market.

## Day Care

o     a lack of affordable, quality day care within reasonable travel distance from work and home.

o     day care subsidies that are insufficient to meet the demand.

## Support Services

o     few specialized services (such as hot lines, support groups, legal advocacy clinics) exist for the assaulted woman.

We all know that there are not enough resources to meet the demands. Social conditions will only improve with strong political actions. In the meanwhile, workers can ease the harsh realities an assaulted woman faces by recognizing the impact their attitudes will have on her. The following examples reflect attitudes that hinder and help the assaulted woman's progress.

Police*

**A woman calls the police to request assistance with her violent husband.**

Unhelpful response:     Her call is not given priority. When the officers arrive, much later, it is clear they do not take her situation seriously. One officer, in front of the victim, says to the offender, "come on now, calm down. You know what women are like. What did she do anyway?"

Helpful response:     Her call is received with respect and concern for her safety. She is believed. The officers arrive promptly - one meets with her to assess her safety and finds out what she wants to do (e.g., be taken to the local shelter). The other officer meets with the offender and informs him that, "it is illegal to hit your wife regardless of what she's done. It is your responsibility to control your temper. As assault charge can be laid against you."

---

*     As of 1983, the police in Ontario were instructed to treat wife-beating as a crime and to initiate laying charges as they would in a stranger assault.

## Doctor

**A woman tells her doctor that her nerves are shot.**

Unhelpful response:
The doctor is busy and unwilling to probe behind the patient's presenting request. She is handed a prescription for Valium and is patronizingly patted on her arm as she leaves. "Things will be better in a few days, dear. You just take these and get some rest."

Helpful response:
The doctor responds with obvious concern and asks her to tell more about her situation. It is learned that her husband has a jealous streak and this clues the doctor in to potential abuse. She is asked directly, "Has your husband ever harmed you?" Her response guides the doctor in further questions and her right to live with freedom from assault is confirmed.

## Social Worker

**A woman finally gets the courage to tell her social worker about the abuse.**

Unhelpful response:
The social worker listens attentively but knows there are always two sides to the story. Trained to be impartial, the social worker searches for the right response. "Do you think you did or said anything that may have contributed to your husband's outburst?"

Helpful response:
The social worker believes her immediately and tells her so. The woman is assured, "no matter what you did or said, you did not make him violent. He is responsible for his own behaviour."

## Lawyer

**A woman calls her lawyer and says she wants to sue her husband for divorce.**

Unhelpful response:
The lawyer rushes in to process the papers without fully understanding the woman's situation. Later, when the woman hesitates about following through with the advice, she is blamed for wasting the lawyer's time.

Helpful response:
After listening to her story, the lawyer outlines her legal rights, clarifies any misinformation she may have received and encourages her to take time to think about her legal options. The lawyer respects her timing and leaves the door open to future questions or requests she might have when she is ready.

## Clergy

**A woman asks to speak to her minister after the weekly prayer service.**

Unhelpful response:
The minister listens to her story, showing visible signs of discomfort. After all, the minister knows and likes her husband. The minister comments that her husband must be under severe stress. "Are you sure that you're being as patient and loving to him as you can be?"

| | |
|---|---|
| Helpful response: | The minister is sensitive to her obvious embarrassment and tries to make her comfortable. After hearing her story, the minister shows visible alarm about her being subjected to such cruelty. She is assured that "no one should have to tolerate that," and goes on to assess her immediate safety. |

## Marriage Counsellor

**A couple comes in together for an interview. The wife has obvious signs of physical injury.**

| | |
|---|---|
| Unhelpful response: | The marriage counsellor insists on interviewing the couple together. Although the woman's injury is noted, the marriage counsellor focuses primarily on poor communication patterns between the couple. The couple is urged to verbalize their stresses. "I won't be able to help you unless you are willing to speak frankly." |
| Helpful response: | The marriage counsellor quickly notes the wife's physical condition. Each spouse is interviewed separately to assess the situation. The primary focus of the interview is to ensure the wife's safety and to refer for medical attention. |

## The Psychological Experience of the Victim

**Fear** is the most predominant feeling that surfaces when working with an assault victim. It rules her actions and colours her every waking moment. It even intrudes and plays havoc with her sleep patterns, causing insomnia and recurrent nightmares. This sleep disruption may lead to dependence on addictive sleeping aids such as sleeping pills, tranquilizers. Her partner is likely to have threatened her with bodily harm or death if she attempts to break the silence or worse, if she considers leaving him. It is not uncommon to hear women tell stories such as:

> My husband threatened he would kill me with his bare hands if he ever got wind of my plans to leave him. He says, "If you leave me, I'll find you. No matter how long it takes, I'll track you down. You can't get away from me. When I find you you'll wish you were dead. I'll destroy that pretty face so no one will ever want you. I'll not only kill you but I'll destroy anyone who helps you get away from me. I'll kill you, the children and then I'll take my own life."

It is very important for the worker to uncover these threats and assess their harmfulness. Many times clients have told me of their desire to reach out for help but fear his threats to harm anyone who intervenes. Many would rather contain the violence in their own home than possibly jeopardize anyone else's safety, which is a tribute to their bravery. Although some people might consider this trait of self-sacrifice as martyrdom or masochism, it really reflects their concern for others' safety. Traditional female role conditioning prepares women well for this position of self-sacrifice. They get the message very early on that they must always put others ahead of themselves in order to fulfill their role of nurturer and care-taker. Our role is to assist them to be as caring, concerned and protective of themselves as they often are for others. Many are immobilized by their terror. It is often the underlying reason why they remain where they are. To deal with the ever-present fear, many deny the horror of the violence and threats and minimize their need for safety.

## Minimizing the Abuse

Most assaulted women, especially in their first contact with a professional, tend to minimize the extent and severity of the abuse. The underlying thinking of this minimization includes:

1. Her fear that talking about it may make her situation worse.

Can I trust this professional?
Will I be believed?
Will I be blamed?
What will be done with the information?

2. Her lack of accurate information about what abuse is and who is victim to it.

"He's never left a mark on me. I'm not a battered woman."
"I thought it only happened to people on welfare. My husband is a doctor."

3. Her need to believe that "It's not so bad" as a means of coping with her life until she's ready to deal with the reality and take protective action. This distancing is a useful defense, given she is still living within the danger. This phenomenon is not unique to assaulted women. Most people -- police, fire-fighters, hostages -- in high-risk positions use distancing as a survival technique.

4. Her shame and embarrassment about the abuse.

"This kind of thing only happens to other people, not me."

5. Her belief that she is responsible for the abuse.

"If I could just be a better wife."
"After all, I'm the one who married him."

## Isolation

The assaulted woman has little access to a personal support network. Her fears for the safety of her loved ones keep her quiet. Her shame and embarrassment over the beatings keep her at arm's length from others. The few friends or acquaintances in her life are unlikely to know about the reign of terror in her home. Even if she attempts to reach out, her partner often sabotages her efforts by controlling her activities and limiting any contacts outside of the marriage. He may deliberately alienate her family and friends by rude and obnoxious behaviour.

She is unlikely to have any positive connections to rewarding work, child-care relief or esteem-building educational, recreational or therapeutic activities. Her social isolation limits her opportunities for realistic feedback that might modify her perceptions of her situation. Her loneliness then serves to increase her dependence on her partner, the very person who promotes the isolation. The cycle is complete. She is forced to accept his definition of her value as a person.

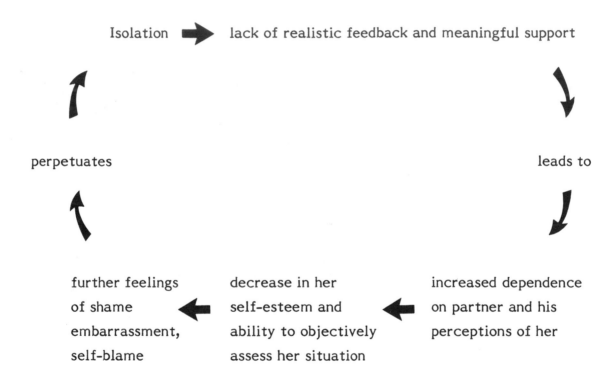

## Helplessness

The assaulted woman is often in a state of "learned helplessness," a phenomenon described in detail by Walker.[2] This means her attempts to control, escape or avoid the violence have been unsuccessful. It brings about a sense of powerlessness that leads to a belief that nothing she does will change her situation.

---

[2] Walker, Lenore. The Battered Woman. New York: Harper and Row, 1979.

Numerous psychological experiments on various animals have been tested to illustrate this phenomenon. For example, Seligman and his colleagues placed dogs in cages and applied shocks at unpredictable intervals.[3] The dogs quickly learned that no matter what they did they could not control the shocks. They lost their spirit and showed visible signs of apathy and listlessness. Passive subservience and compliance marked their character. Even when the cage door was opened, they did not escape. It was as if they had lost their will to live. To counter the effects of the experiment, repeated efforts of dragging the dogs out of the cage were necessary before the dogs learned they could master their situation again. Assaulted women describe a similar experience -- a lack of control that eventually leads to a chronic state of helplessness, hopelessness and utter despair. The longer the woman is exposed to the abuse, the longer it will take her to overcome the effects of the helplessness. Even though she may have initiated contact with you, it is important to understand that she may think you will be as helpless as she is to change the situation. She sees her partner as all-powerful. You may have to convince her that you can help her change her situation. Until now, nothing has worked.

## Internalizes Blame

The assaulted woman is not unusual. Like many of us, she believes the myths about violence in the home. She often believes she is to blame, and that she provokes the violence in the home. She thinks she caused the beating because she did something wrong. Her partner asks her repeatedly, "Why do you make me hit you? If you would just do what you're told, this would never happen." She tries to become more perfect, **not** realizing that the violence has little to do with her behaviour or personality.

Victim thinking is built into the female role. She grows up believing it is her responsibility to make the marriage work; if her husband mistreats her, then it must be **her** that is doing something wrong. She gets a lot of support for this belief from her family, friends, professionals and the community. She spends much of her time and energy planning her life and her conversations so she does not upset her husband. This existence is often described as "walking on egg shells." Her feelings of guilt for his violence take him off the hook and perpetuate his use of violence with little or no repercussions.

## Ambivalence

The violent partner is not violent all the time. There may be long periods when

---

[3] Seligman, Martin. _Helplessness_. W.H. Freeman, 1975.

she feels he is a kind and loving husband. This is the crux of her ambivalence. She wants the violence to end, but not the marriage. She **hopes** he will change. She wants to believe his promises. She thinks she loves him. Her definition of love may be different from ours, but it is hers we must pay attention to.

She is also terrified of the prospect of being on her own. Separation from her spouse may bring radical changes in her lifestyle. If she has been at home full-time raising her children, she may have to give this up, find a job and turn her kids over to a day-care centre, or she may be forced onto public assistance. For a middle or upper class woman, the drop in standard of living may be dramatic. She may face the harshest adjustments in the event of separation.

These are real barriers to change, not just for assaulted women, but for most women in our society. Very few women in unhappy marriages -- violent or not --have the financial independence to leave their marriages without concerns for supporting themselves and their children. Women who work outside the home still earn on the average only 60% of what a man earns.

## Internalization of Oppression[4]

When any group believes it is inferior and deserves to be treated badly, this makes it easier for the bad treatment to continue. Such beliefs are sometimes called "internalization of oppression." Messages about inferiority may come from a variety of sources -- family and friends, children's story books, school books, advertisements and movies. A first experience of victimization becomes complicated when the victim internalizes her oppression.

The abused woman may already see herself as inferior and when she is first assaulted this may act to confirm her suspicion that "something is wrong with me." The woman who has little support in challenging the traditional female role is most vulnerable to remaining in an abusive relationship. The greater her internalization of her oppression, the longer it will take her to overcome her victimization.

## Low Self-Esteem

The end result of repeated abuse and victimization is a battered self-esteem. The woman's sense of worthiness, self-confidence and belief in her abilities have all been damaged. Most humiliating for her is that she has been beaten by the person she chose to be her husband, the person who was supposed to love,

---

[4] Adapted from Ruitort, Monica and Shirley Endicott Small. Working With Assaulted Immigrant Women: A Handbook For Lay Counsellors. Toronto: Education Wife Assault, 1984.

honour and cherish her. She often describes this as her severest blow -- the ultimate betrayal.

The more severe the abuse is and the longer it has gone on, the poorer self-image she will have. She begins to believe the names he calls her -- stupid, incompetent, ugly and so on.

In the past, she may have threatened to leave or actually fled for a brief time, resolving never to return unless her partner changes. Once on her own, her fears and the cold reality of her single life overwhelm her. Her options are limited and she feels **forced** to return to an unchanged situation. Her inability to sustain her resolutions of a life without her husband results in more self-blame and lowered self-esteem. She feels beaten once again, and knows her defeat spells victory for her husband.

The woman who **voluntarily** returns to her husband because he has promised to change (e.g., he is attending a men's group) can at least feel some measure of control over her life. She is able to return with greater integrity. She has clearly demonstrated to her partner that she is only prepared to be with him if he proves he has changed his abusive behaviour.

Hope

The woman hopes her husband will change and become the husband of her dreams. It is important to convey respect for her dreams of a happy marriage and a good life. She is not unusual. We all have our dreams.

Too often we blame the victim by focusing on questions such as "Why does she stay?", again implying there is something wrong with her. We need to view her in a more positive light. It is more helpful to think of her as a courageous woman who survives despite the many obstacles placed in her way. In other words, we should be asking, "Where does she find the strength to leave a violent relationship in the face of such odds?"

# 3 WHY MEN ASSAULT THEIR WIVES

It is not clearly understood why certain men choose to assault their wives and other men choose not to. Experienced workers in this area have, however, reached consensus on three factors that contribute to a man's use of violence against his wife.

1. Certain societal conditions and beliefs encourage violence.

2. Certain responses from the community will perpetuate violence.

3. Certain psychological characteristics are common among offenders who use violence.

## Societal Conditions and Beliefs Encourage Violence Against Wives

### Social Tolerance

There is tremendous social tolerance for men to use physical force against their wives. An example of this tolerance is demonstrated in an experiment by Shotland and Shaw, who tested bystanders' reactions to a man attacking a woman.[1] Observers were much more reluctant to intervene when they believed the couple to be married than when they thought they were strangers. The message men receive is ambiguous: "We may not think it is good for you to be violent; but if you are violent, especially to your wife, we won't interfere." Men continue to assault their wives because no one stops them.

### Historical Rights

In our male-dominated society, men have historically been assigned the task of upholding a hierarchical structure within the family as well as within the community. When this structure was challenged or threatened, it was husbands and fathers who were expected to deal with it, even if that meant using physical force to keep family members in line. Remember the history of the Rule of Thumb.

### Beliefs and Values

Men born into this system and socialized in the traditional male role came to believe the following ideas, which promote the continuation of wife assault:

---

[1]   Shotland, R.L., and M.K. Shaw. "Bystanders Response to an Assault: When a Man Attacks a Woman." Journal of Personality and Social Psychology. Vol. 34, No. 5, 1976.

1.    The superiority of men.

2.    The equation of physical power and dominance with masculinity.

3.    The validity of using physical force and intimidation as a problem-solving method.[2]

## Community Responses Perpetuate Violence Against Wives

A community's allocation of resources will reflect its stand on social issues. As we have already seen, there are limited community resources available to the victim. The attitudes she confronts from most segments of the community are more often than not detrimental to ensuring her safety. Offenders also face a dismal shortage of effective resources. They also confront responses from the community that fail to hold them accountable for their violent behaviour. **For every victim blamed, there is an offender excused.** The offender's life is complicated by a number of factors, such as:

1.    There are limited resources and programs available of the types needed to help him change his behaviour, such as hot lines staffed by ex-offenders, men's groups and court-mandated programs.

2.    Very few professionals have attitudes that will facilitate changing men's attitudes.

3.    His family and friends often make excuses for his behaviour.

4.    Society and its institutions often condone his behaviour through an unwillingness to take his violence seriously.

All of these factors make it doubly difficult for him to change.

## The Psychological Profile of the Violent Man

### Denial

Most violent men do not believe they have a problem. They tend to minimize, omit important details and even lie about the frequency and severity of the violence. Denying the violence gets him off the hook for his behaviour and thus he does not have to change himself. He also denies it in order to avoid the legal consequences of his behaviour. Denial protects him from evaluating the reality of his life.

This defense may have been developed early on in his life as a way to cope with punitive childhood experiences. It acts as a defense to ward off his depression and anxiety. The threat of her departure painfully confronts him

---

[2]    Carlson, Bonnie. "Battered Women and Their Assailants." Social Work. November, 1977.

with himself and the consequences of his violence. He becomes desperate and is often at a loss to cope. It is at the point of separation from his partner that he is most vulnerable to suicidal or homicidal behaviour. He should not be left to fend for himself. He does not know how. At this stage, he is most amenable to immediate crisis intervention. He is less well-defended, thus more open to change. A worker would be wise to reach out to him at this time.

## Externalized Blame

Most offenders do not hold themselves responsible for their violent behaviour. They believe they are driven to it by external forces beyond their control. They have endless lists of reasons, justifications and rationalizations as to why they had to act violently. Some of the common excuses given are:

> "She just wouldn't let up on me. I had to hit her to keep her quiet."

> "She was giving me the silent treatment. I had to shake her out of it."

> "I guess I drank too much. I didn't know what I was doing. I've really been under a lot of pressure lately. She should know not to bug me."

## Dependency Fears

Most violent men are terrified of losing their wives. They depend on their wives to meet all of their emotional needs. They unrealistically expect that their primary relationship will fill the emptiness in their lives. They lack empathy for their partners and are unable to see their wives' needs as separate from their own. Their often repressed fear of losing her causes them to be easily threatened by outside influences. This results in excessive jealousies and possessive, controlling behaviour. Down deep they sense they are losing her, so they cling even tighter, ironically forcing her further away.

## Internalization of the Traditional Male Role

He grows up believing he should be the "head of the household," that his word is the most important and that he is the ultimate authority. He often accepts this definition of men without question! He learns early on that to show emotion is a weakness. Men are supposed to be strong, in control, aggressive and successful. He believes he owns and is responsible for his wife. She is a reflection of him and he feels justified to take the necessary steps to make her comply with what he wants. To be in control means to control her and to totally dominate her life. If this cannot be accomplished by force of will, he will resort to "force of fist." The more he adheres to this rigid definition of masculinity, the more likely he is to use force to get his own way. His children are often viewed in the same way. As many as one third of abusive husbands abuse their children as well as their wives.[3]

## Most Emotions are Expressed as Anger

Most of his fears and anxieties are masked under the guise of "manly behaviour." Anger is an acceptable masculine feeling. He is unable to articulate a range of feelings. He relies on his wife to take care of all the feelings in the family. His language is limited to feeling "fine" or "furious." Words such as annoyed, frustrated, hurt, disappointed, sad and lonely are not a part of his vocabulary. He has been trained to be action- and problem-oriented rather than process-oriented. This makes him particularly vulnerable in discussions of an intimate nature, since he has little ability to express his feelings. He is easily threatened by his partner's skill at emotional expression. He copes with his inadequacy by "physically shutting her up." Although many things and people in his life make him angry, the brunt of his anger is directed at his wife. The majority of men know they would not get away with harming someone outside of the family.

## Isolation

For violent men, isolation from others tends to be self-imposed. He distrusts his environment and most people in it. He may appear to have many friends but the friendships are of a superficial nature. He seldom discloses anything important. He expects to solve his problems in private. Asking for help or expecting support from others (except from his partner) is seen as unmanly and weak.

He is often seen as a "nice guy," but he keeps people at arm's length. The only person who really knows him is his wife. This often accounts for people's disbelief when they hear of his violence. It seems out of character from the side he has shown to the world. It is this side that women fall in love with --the Dr. Jekyll part. Mr. Hyde is reserved for private encounters with his wife. His convincing, charming manner and the fact that there are usually no witnesses to his violence makes him credible in the community.

## Control Issues

**Poor impulse control.** Some men are so detached from their feelings they are oblivious to their mounting rage. They are often described by others as a walking time-bomb but fail to see this in themselves. Suddenly they explode!

---

[3]    Walker, Lenore. The Battered Woman. New York: Harper and Row, 1979.

They are often more surprised by their violent outbursts than those around them. The triggering event seems trivial in light of their reaction. When later analyzing the events leading up to the violent outburst, they state they felt out of control. The violence was an attempt to ward off their increasing anxiety and to regain control of the situation. Because they acted so impulsively they did not consider the consequences of their behaviour.

**Excessive, rigid control.** Some men have the opposite of poor impulse control. They know exactly what they are doing. They plan their attacks. They decide in advance where to strike the victim and how much force to apply to accomplish their goal. The goal, of course, is to induce fear in order to control her behaviour. These men seldom come for counselling. When they do, they are much more difficult to work with because they seldom feel remorse for what they've done. These men are particularly dangerous and their partners are often forced to go into hiding if they want to leave them.

## Childhood Experience of Violence

Most violent men in counselling have experienced violence in their own homes of origin. Some studies have found that as many as 81% of men who assault their wives have grown up in a violent home.[4] They have watched helplessly as their father beat their mother. Powerless to effectively intervene, they may also have been abused themselves. They grow up believing adults are not to be trusted. They view the world as a hostile and unsafe place. Obviously, this experience is not conducive to a positive self-image. Under stress, they resort to the same tactics used by their parents. They have **learned** to be violent.

The offender who was not exposed to violence in his home still learns early in his life that to be male is to be aggressive. Exposure to violent competitive sports (hockey, football, boxing), schoolyard fights (where to be passive is to risk being called a "sissy"), advertisements (Brut -- a perfume for "real men") and television brainwash boys into believing that violence is a natural, inevitable part of malehood.

## Low Self-Esteem

The offender feels powerless in his life. He is often described as a "nice guy." He'd give you the shirt off his back. He is unable to take care of himself and is easily taken advantage of. He swallows his feelings, ignores small resentments and generally feels impotent in his life. Each time he is violent, his self-esteem gets further eroded and makes him feel worse.

---

[4] Roy, Maria (ed.). The Abusive Partner: An Analysis of Domestic Battering. New York: Van Nostrand Reinhold, 1980.

Violence is used as a last, desperate attempt to bring the situation into their control. Unfortunately, in the short term it seems to work. He gets immediate satisfaction from striking out, a physical release of pent up tension and his wife's compliance. In the long run, it is ineffective because he eventually drives his wife away out of fear for her life. Remorse and guilt is often felt after an incident and can lead to a "honeymoon" period. Most men seen in counselling do not feel good about what they have done.

## PART TWO    INTRODUCTION TO INTERVENTION

A crisis is a time when individuals face an insurmountable obstacle that temporarily disorganizes their life.  Their normal coping mechanisms fail to prevent the upheaval.  A period of upset, chaos and confusion usually follows.  They are at a turning point in their life.  People in crisis react with increased vulnerability and heightened potential.  It is the counsellor's task to promote growth while enhancing self-esteem.

---

### THE GOALS OF CRISIS INTERVENTION

#### VICTIM
The goal is to provide **just enough** information
and support to mobilize her to take protective action.

#### OFFENDER
The goal is to encourage him to take responsibility
for stopping his violent behaviour.

#### CHILDREN
The goal is to ensure their immediate safety.

---

### Intake Procedures:   Identifying the Crisis

Asking about violence must be a standard part of any initial contact with a client.  If you are in an agency setting, the intake worker must be trained to ask routinely about the presence of violence, including suicidal gestures.

Preparation must be made to assist the intake person to practice asking about violence in a way that is comfortable yet still obtains the needed information.  Flexibility in personal style in encouraged.  Samples of questions might be:

o    Has anyone in your family ever hurt themselves or someone else?

o    Is anyone in your family in danger at the present time?

o    Has your partner ever shoved, slapped or threatened to harm you?

o    How do people in your family fight?

o      Does anyone in your family use force to get their own way?

If the intake worker senses some hesitation, she might say something like, "The reason I ask is because of my concern for your safety and to find out if you should talk to a counsellor immediately. What you tell me is totally confidential."

Most clients will talk about the violence when asked, but some may need this extra probing and assurance that the information will be handled in a sensitive way.

Although workers often express doubts about directly questioning for the presence of violence, few, if any, clients have expressed distress about this line of questioning. In fact, many clients (even those where there is no violence present) have expressed relief and gratitude for the worker's concern about their safety, a secondary gain that enhances the counselling bond.

Once violence has been identified, the intake worker passes the call to an ongoing worker. **Priority should always be given to high-risk situations.**

In those agencies where there has been a process for consistently identifying the presence of violence (e.g., Vancouver Family Service Association, Family Service Association of Metropolitan Toronto) the statistics have risen substantially.

**Signs and Symptoms of Wife Assault**

In your contact with any family members, the following observations should be considered clues to the possibility of wife assault:

Husbands

o      a history of wife assault or child abuse in his family for origin.

o      a suspicion of child abuse or sexual abuse in his role as a father.

o      abuse of drugs or alcohol.

o      a history of suicidal thoughts or suicide attempts.

o      such characteristics as impulsiveness, temper tantrums, jealousy, possessiveness, excessive dependence on his wife or immaturity.

o      rigid views of men and women.

Wives

o      chronic complaints of poor health.

o      frequent visits to a doctor.

o      use of tranquilizers and/or abuse of alcohol.

o    a history of suicidal thoughts or actions.

o    a suspicion of child abuse in her role as a mother.

o    sleeping difficulties (i.e., insomnia, violent nightmares).

o    severe agitation, anxiety or obvious nervousness.

o    confused thinking, inability to make decisions, lack of eye contact.

o    rigid views of men and women.

Children

o    aggressive behaviour (particularly in boys).

o    withdrawing, passive, clinging behaviour (particularly in girls and young children).

o    victims of child abuse/sexual abuse.

o    a suspicion of parent abuse or sibling abuse.

o    night-time difficulties, such as insomnia, nightmares, bedwetting, problems with bedtime.

o    somatic complaints, such as headaches, stomach-aches, chronic colds, allergies.

o    self-destructive, accident-prone behaviour.

o    acting-out escapist behaviour (particularly in teenagers) such as running away, drug/alcohol abuse, prostitution, pregnancy, early marriage.

**What To Do If You Do Not Know There Is Violence**

Ideally the presence of violence should be screened at the point of intake. However, in reality, this does not always happen. This next section discusses three different types of situations and how to probe for violence in each of them.

A Woman Comes In Alone*

What does she identify as the problem? Do you know from the intake form whether violence is present and to what extent? If not, ask her directly about

---

*    Although it is unusual for a man to come in alone identifying his violent temper as a problem, when one does half the battle is won. Most men who seek help on their own do so under other guises (e.g., seeking help for depression, drinking problems, work-related problems, problems with their wives). The counsellor must probe for the use of violence, which may well be the root of his problems. Even though he may deny he has a problem with violence, do not rule it out prematurely. It may take some time to uncover.

the possibility of abuse. Once you know that violence is present, you must find out what kind of assistance she is requesting.

Does she want you to have contact with her husband? What are her plans for the relationship? Does she want her husband to know she is seeing a counsellor? Based on her answers, you will decide on how to proceed. If she is still living with her husband but is firm in her conviction to leave him, your counselling must focus on helping her make a realistic plan for separation. Your goal is to help her stop being a victim, **not** to keep the marriage together. If, on the other hand, she wants to stay married but end the violence, it is imperative you see her husband and assess his willingness to change. **Working with her will not end his violence.**

Even if the woman decides to leave the marriage, ask her permission to interview her husband at least once. Do this to assess his threats and capacity for violence. This will give you a more realistic picture of her situation. The counsellor's contact with the offender lets him know that the violence is now public and thus increases her safety. It also give the counsellor the opportunity to offer some help to the offender. If he does **not** get some form of intervention counselling or legal, he is likely to assault women in any future relationships. If you are able to motivate the offender to get help, it is probably wiser to refer him to his own separate counsellor, unless you sense the couple may reconcile. In that case, it is possible for the counsellor to work with both the victim and the offender. Even if reconciliation occurs, individual work with each spouse is necessary until her safety is firmly established.

## A Couple Comes In Together

What do they identify as the problem? Do you know from the intake form whether there violence is present and to what extent? Does she seem intimidated by her partner's presence? Does she seem fearful or anxious? Indicators might be her silence, compliance or passivity. Does he seem overbearing? Does he seem disrespectful of women? Does he try to control the direction of the interview? If you suspect there is the possibility of abuse, take time to see each of them individually. One way to introduce this into the interview is by suggesting in an authoritative manner:

> I want to spend a few minutes with each of you alone.
> It gives me a chance to get to know each of you as
> individuals outside of your marriage. Joe, how about
> getting a coffee in the waiting room and I'll come and
> get you when I finish speaking with Nancy.

If you discover that there is violence, you must quickly assess the urgency of the situation. If there has been some violence but it is **not** of a crisis nature at present, find out what the woman wants in the way of counselling. Will it be safe for her if you raise this issue in front of the husband? If she is fearful or hesitant it is best to work with the couple in separate interviews until the risk is eliminated. Her safety must always be the priority!

## A Family Comes In Together

What do they identify as the problem? Sometimes it might be a child having problems in school, a rebellious teenager, a child with eating problems or a sickly child. Use some of the same assessment observations and questions outlined in the couple interview. Make a point of spending about ten minutes alone with each family member. Depending on the ages of the children, you may want to see them together as a group. See the mother first, as she often acts as the emotional barometer in the family. Find out from her if she or the children have been abused. This is a good time to check for sexual abuse of the children as well. Again, her response will guide you in your interview with the husband. If she does **not** want you to discuss the abuse with him, then don't! **She knows best.** Set up a separate interview with her at another time.

In your talk with the children, ask them their opinion about what's good in the family and what's not so good. Do they feel safe? How do they fight in their family? Does anyone in their family scare them? Has anyone ever touched them in a bad way? (The use of dolls is an effective way to demonstrate "good touches" and "bad touches.") Were they told not to say anything about certain family secrets? If you have reason to question the children's safety, you must contact the Children's Aid Society immediately. It is an asset to have a sympathetic child-welfare resource to discuss your concerns with. This kind of cooperation ensures that any plan of action undertaken will maximize the safety of all family members.

## 4  COUNSELLING THE ASSAULTED WOMAN

To help assaulted women, counsellors and advocates must first examine their own values and beliefs. The following list has been developed by Barbara Pressman and reflects the values and beliefs necessary for effectively intervening with victims of wife assault. It has been adapted for the purpose of this manual.

1.      No behaviour of any woman justifies or provokes violence. No woman ever deserves to be hit, shoved, kicked or physically hurt in any way.

2.      Women are not masochistic and in no way do they derive any pleasure from being physically hurt or threatened.

3.      A major contributing factor to women remaining in violent relationships is the endorsement and teaching by our social institutions that women belong in the home, are less competent than men to succeed in the work force, should defer to the dominance of their husbands and should be the primary emotional support of the family.

4.      In counselling, the problems of the marital relationship cannot be the initial focus. Until all family members are safe, it is too dangerous to discuss problems of the family or the relationship other than the violence.

5.      Anyone working with assaulted women must provide role models of competent, successful, assertive women. They must confront and challenge the belief of many assaulted women that they are responsible for the violence and help assaulted women develop a sense of themselves as competent and able to make decisions and choices. By allowing each assaulted woman to make decisions and respecting those decisions even when those decisions are not the ones counsellors would make for themselves, counsellors can powerfully indicate their belief in the woman's strength.[1]

Can male counsellors be as effective with assaulted women as female counsellors? Generally speaking, no. Feedback, not only from assaulted women but also from male counsellors, suggests that male counsellors may encounter problems that female counsellors would not. For example, assaulted women are often intimidated by men, distrustful of men and compliant to men's wishes. Their feelings for their abusive partner may be generalized to all men at different stages of the therapeutic process. This is not only a natural response to their victimization but also appears to be an inevitable stage that most assaulted women pass through. A male counsellor, by virtue of his gender, may

---

[1]      Pressman, Barbara. Family Violence Origins and Treatment. University of Guelph: Ontario, 1984.

impede this process, particularly in the crisis stage. However, there are always exceptions. If an assaulted woman does not have access to a female counsellor who shares this value orientation, a male counsellor who does would be the better choice. In this case, value orientation takes precedence over gender.

## Crisis Intervention with the Assaulted Woman

There are two primary tasks at this stage of intervention. They are: creating an atmosphere of trust and respect; and dealing with the practical aspects of the crisis.

To create an atmosphere of trust and respect with the assaulted woman, a counsellor must:

o    Assure her that you believe her story.

o    Let her know she is not the only person this happens to.

o    Inspire her confidence in your skills. Let her know of your experience and your belief that this problem can be solved. This will begin her process of turning despair into hope for change.

o    Validate her feelings and experience. Help her to mobilize her inner resources to deal with the immediate crisis.

o    Focus her energies. She may tend to ramble, to be disjointed in her thinking or to be overwhelmed by her own story.

o    Keep your message clear and simple (e.g., her safety and her children's is your first priority).

o    Give her realistic feedback based on what she's told you.

**Stay calm** even if you feel overwhelmed by her story, do **not** show it. She needs to believe in your strength. You are there to contain her anxiety and fears.

This chapter and the next present questions designed to explore the extent of the problem. They are not meant to bombard the assaulted woman and thus run the risk of alienating her. They are to be used sensitively to gather just enough information to maximize her safety and protection. As workers we sometimes assume we know what's going on in the client's life. Sometimes her reality is quite different than what we would expect.

These questions have several purposes. They get her to begin thinking about her situation realistically and get her to take responsibility for her own safety. They allow you to clarify and correct inaccurate information she may have been told. Finally, they increase your understanding of her unique situation so that your subsequent interventions will reflect heightened awareness.

Dealing with the practical aspects of the crisis includes six steps:

1. Assess the immediate danger to the assaulted woman and her children.

2. Assess her need for medical attention.

3. Determine her access to resources.

4. Assess her need for emergency housing.

5. Refer her to a sympathetic lawyer.

6. Establish ongoing contact.

### 1. Assess Her Immediate Danger

**Physical Safety**

QUESTIONS: **Where is she calling from?  Is she safe?  Where is her partner? Where are her children?  Are they safe?**

PURPOSES:  Establishing her whereabouts will guide you in the urgency of the situation.  If she is at home and her husband is there as well, threatening her, immediate police intervention is required.  Get her address and name and call the police -- immediately!  If she is safe at a friend's home, you have the luxury of getting a fuller picture of the situation to guide your interventions.

**Description of Violence**

QUESTIONS: **Has he threatened her?  What are the threats?  Has he ever carried out his threats in the past?  How is he violent towards her?  Does he kick, hit, shove, choke?  Does he use instruments, objects, weapons to harm her? Does he own a gun?  What kind?**

PURPOSES:  Assessing the frequency and severity of the violence will enable you to measure the lethality of her situation.  Asking questions related to the frequency will help you discover the pattern of the violence and will tell you how much time you have to intervene.  For example, I once had a woman call me on a Friday afternoon at 4:30 p.m.  I had to assess quickly if she needed protection prior to the weekend or if could she wait until Monday for an interview.  In her case, the pattern was fairly clear:  her husband abused her routinely the first Friday of every month.  He would get paid, stop off at a bar for a few, and then come home irate and beat her.  **It was the first Friday of the month.**  Obviously I had to intervene immediately and find her a place for temporary protection.  However, if it was the Monday after the abuse there would likely be more time to help the woman carve out her plan of action.

**Brief Description of the Offender**

QUESTIONS: **Does he abuse drugs or alcohol?  Is he presently sober or drunk?**

Is he suicidal?  Has he ever attempted suicide?  Is he respectful of the law?  Is he violent outside the family?  Does he have a psychiatric history?  What is his emotional state at present?  Does he have medical problems?  Does he abuse the children?

PURPOSES:  You want to find out how dangerous this man is -- to her, to the children, to you, to the police, to the general public, to himself.  Even though the majority of men who assault their wives are not violent outside the home, you need to find out if he is the exception.  If his violence is directed at random, it is possible you are dealing with someone with a psychiatric past or a medical history.  If he is not fearful of the law, the police should know that before they intervene.  They are likely to be in need of protection themselves.  Remember that you are relying on her assessment of the offender, which may not always be reliable, given her intimidation and fear of him.  However, it's the best you've got, so if you err, err on the side of being overly cautious (but calmly so).

## Brief Description of the Victim

QUESTIONS: Does she abuse alcohol or drugs?  Is she presently sober?  Does she have health problems?  Does she have a psychiatric history?  Is she suicidal?  Has she attempted suicide in the past?  What is her emotional state at present?

PURPOSES:  You need to know if she is able to carry out the options presented to her.  That is why you must assess her suicidal tendencies, degree of depression/helplessness -- in essence, her ability to act!  You want to connect with this woman just enough to get her mobilized into protective action.  You don't want her life story at this stage, so keep her focussed by firmly drawing out just the details you need to make the appropriate decisions.

## Brief Description of the Children

QUESTIONS: Are the children in danger?  Has he ever directed his violence towards them?  Has he sexually abused them?  Have they tried to stop his abuse by intervening?  How have they handled the violence?  Are they close to their dad, their mom?  Gently probe to find out if she has been abusive to them.  What does she think the kids know about the abuse?

PURPOSES:  You need to assess the impact of violence on the children and their ability to cope with a possible separation.  In most cases, it is wisest for her to take the children with her.  Advise her to take along their favourite toy, blanket or teddy.  This could save a lot of upset when bedtime comes and they need comfort from their familiar friend.

2.    <u>Assess Her Need For Medical Attention</u>

QUESTIONS: **When did the assault occur? Do you have any injuries (bruises, cuts, aches, cracked or broken limbs, headaches, blurred vision)? Have you had medical attention? Do you feel comfortable telling your doctor about the assault?**

PURPOSES: Assessing the consequences of the assault will help her avoid further minimization. Probing for specific details will help you assess the need for medical attention. Encourage her to meet with her doctor (or a doctor you can recommend) even if the injuries seem superficial. Do this for three reasons: 1. Sometimes internal injuries occur that might go unnoticed. 2. The doctor will be able to document the assault, which can then be used as evidence in the event of legal action. 3. Her doctor will gain a better understanding of her situation once she or he knows of the facts. People can't help what they can't see. Violence must be made public. Encourage her to avoid hiding. Reinforce the fact that it is **not** her fault. She has nothing to be ashamed about. If people blame her, that's a reflection of their ignorance, **not** her weakness. Remember, **publicity is protection.** The more people who know the facts of her situation, the more likely she is to receive effective assistance. And her personal support system will broaden!

3.    <u>Determine Her Access To Resources</u>

QUESTIONS: **Who knows about the violence? Do you have family or friends who can support you right now? Do you have any money, credit cards, access to personal or joint bank accounts? Do you have access to immediate transportation?**

PURPOSES: Practical discussion of her own resources will increase her sense of personal power and will let you know clearly what she needs in the way of concrete aids.

4.    <u>Assess The Need For Emergency Housing</u>

QUESTIONS: **Are you in danger if you stay in your own home? Could you stay with your family or friends? Would you be safe with them? Do you know what a shelter is? Would you consider staying there temporarily for safety until you sort out your options?**

PURPOSES: A shelter is **not** necessarily the best place for every assaulted woman. Remaining in her own home and having her husband court-ordered to leave is **not** always the safest option either. Staying with a neighbour or relative may also be unsafe if the husband will look there first. Each woman's situation is unique. Knowing her ability to cope with chaos (inevitable in shelter life), knowing her husband's degree of respect for the law (a court order to keep him out may be very effective), knowing her friends' and family's level of support (what if they pressure her to go back?), are all important points to consider when assessing the need for emergency shelter and its whereabouts.

## 5.    Refer Her To A Sympathetic Lawyer

QUESTIONS: **Do you have a lawyer?  Is s/he sympathetic to your situation? Does s/he have a good understanding about wife assault?  Do you feel comfortable confiding in your lawyer?  Do you know what your legal rights are? Have you ever taken legal action in the past to protect yourself?  Have the police ever been called to your home?  What did they do?  Was their intervention helpful?  Would you call them again?**

PURPOSES:  Good legal advice is essential.  Many assaulted women have little factual knowledge about their legal rights.  Often, their partners have filled them with misinformation and sometimes outright lies (e.g., "if you leave me you'll be charged with desertion" or "you will lose the children if you leave").  A woman should **never** be pressured to take legal action.  She is vulnerable to your influence, so she may agree to start legal proceedings before she fully comprehends the process and its impact.  She may be indebted to you for your help, so may seek to win your approval by appearing compliant and grateful. My experience tells me that most women who withdrew prematurely from legal actions did so because they had not been fully briefed on the system and thus felt pushed into a process they were not ready for.  Many women share their sense of failure from this.

To avoid this negative experience advise women to have one educational session with a sensitive lawyer who will outline all of her legal rights and options she can take if she so chooses.  This is also an opportunity for the lawyer to clarify misinformation.  This structure removes the pressure from both the lawyer and the client.  She gets a chance to meet her lawyer in a nonthreatening, nonpressured atmosphere.  The lawyer gets a chance to assess her readiness to take legal action.  The woman is then able to leave and think things over carefully before she decides to retain the lawyer or take her/his advice.

## 6.    Establish Ongoing Contact

QUESTIONS:     **Where can you be reached?  Will it be safe for me to call you at home?  Will you give me the name and number of someone you trust in the** event of an emergency (e.g., we're cut off, husband interrupts call)?

PURPOSES:     Establishing ongoing contact gives a clear message that you are concerned about her safety and want to continue helping her sort out her options.  It also serves to reduce the worker's anxiety when you are able to follow up after the crisis and check on her safety.

**Tips For Counsellors/Advocates**

1.     Always keep in mind that although this may be your one hundredth call from a victim in crisis, it may be **her first time** reaching out for help.  By merely being the helper you have a lot of power. Use it wisely.  What you say and how you say it may impact on her life profoundly.  For example, one woman in crisis I spoke with briefly on the phone and had no further contact with called me years later to thank me for my help.  When I asked her what she had found most helpful, she replied, "You took me seriously.  You helped me see I had some power over my future.  I always remembered that.  My life has gotten a lot better since then."

2.     The first time you meet with an assaulted women in an agency setting expect to be with her longer than the therapy hour.  If this is the first time she's shared her story, she needs your individual attention and time to tell it at her own pace and in her own style.  Many first interviews have lasted two to three hours (with breaks).  After the first disclosure, sessions can move back to greater structure (one hour) if there is to be ongoing contact.

3.     Treat your first contact with her as your last.  This may be your only opportunity to get through to her.  Arm her with some self-protective strategies, such as shelter numbers, police number, escape routes.

4.     Phone interviews can be just as effective as face-to-face interviews.  In fact, for some women the anonymity of the phone creates a **safe barrier,** allowing them to speak more freely.

5.     At the end of your contact, get her to repeat back a summary of what she heard you say.  Clarification is a key to successful engagement.  Most of us filter what we hear, so in her anxious state she is unlikely to hear you clearly the first time.  Repetition of important statements is a powerful tool.

6.     As part of closure in your first interview, find out her fears about having shared her story.  What does she imagine you think of her now?  This will give you one final opportunity to reassure her that talking about her victimization is a positive step toward ending it.

7. **Set realistic expectations for yourself as a worker. You** cannot ensure her safety. You can only provide options, so **she** can take responsibility to ensure her own safety. Sometimes in our own fear for her safety, we rescue her rather than empower her. This is an easy trap, especially if the victim appears dependent, confused and outwardly fragile. It may seem expedient to follow the quick route of telling her what to do, but the route with the lasting impact will be the one that facilitates her own independence.

8. **Help her set realistic expectations for herself** (just phoning for information may be tremendous progress for a woman who has been victimized for years). It is important for the counsellor to talk with her about her progress in detail. The assaulted woman is not used to getting realistic feedback nor is she used to being praised for her successes.

9. Respect her timing and her ability to digest the new information you've provided.

10. Stay away from patronizing "should" statements ("you should leave"), from judgemental statements ("you're right, what a brute") or from any statement that may be construed as an order. Remember where she is coming from -- a husband who is likely authoritarian and paternalistic.

11. Only share facts about assault that will lead to the goal of mobilizing her resources to protect herself. For example, she might think she can't leave, even for temporary protection, because the children will be upset. You might let her know that you admire her concern for her children. She is obviously trying very hard to be a conscientious parent. However, is she aware of the impact violence has on children? Then gently lead her into a brief discussion about children and violence. Do **not** overwhelm her with all your knowledge on the issue. Remember that you may be charting completely new territory with her. Perhaps, she has always believed she was doing right by the children to stay at home and put up. Don't be too quick to destroy her beliefs or you might well damage her esteem even further.

12. If you don't understand certain of her actions or thoughts -- **ASK her!** She's the best judge of herself and often has quite sound reasons for doing what she's doing. For example, at the end of a first interview, one client took my business card and put it in the leather sole of her shoe. I asked her why she was doing that and she said, "it is the only place I can hide important papers from my husband." Good strategy!

## Assessment with the Assaulted Woman

After the assaulted woman is safe, plans can be made for ongoing counselling. It is difficult to draw a line between crisis intervention, short-term counselling and long-term counselling. The process of change needs to be viewed on a continuum. Any woman living in a violence-prone environment is always in some degree of danger, in some measure of crisis.

A series of questions will guide you in your work with the assaulted woman. No question should be asked unless it is purposeful. Her responses (both verbal and nonverbal) will assist you in developing a specific plan tailored to her needs. The areas include:

1. Family of Origin

QUESTIONS: **Would she describe her childhood as happy, sad, secure, etc? Did she like herself? What were her relationships like with her mother, her father, her sisters and brothers? What form of discipline was used? How was affection shown? Was there any form of abuse taking place with any family member? Who was the victim? Who was the offender? Was she sexually abused as a child? By whom? When did she leave home and under what circumstances? What were the family messages she received about being a girl? What were her expectations about relationships with men? With women? Were there special factors that influenced her life (such as religious, cultural, geographic influences?) What were her expectations for her future in regards to money, career, education and family?**

PURPOSES:
o     to help connect her childhood experience with her experience as an adult.

o     to help her develop a picture of herself prior to her present relationship.

o     to help her uncover the influences in her past life that form the foundation of her present values and beliefs.

2. Frequency and Severity of the Violence

QUESTIONS: **When did the violence start? Under what circumstances? What is her definition of abuse? How often do the assaults occur? Are there particular triggers to the assaults that she can identify, such as pregnancy, loss of a job, alcohol, her return to the work force? What are the reasons he gives her for the abuse — you nag, you're a lousy mother? Do the assaults get worse over time? What injuries did she sustain? What form of assault occurs -- psychological, physical, sexual, damage to property or pets? Does he abuse the children --physically, psychologically, sexually? Does his violence go beyond the home?**

PURPOSES:

o to help her identify herself as a victim of violence.

o to help her recognize the pattern of abuse.

o to help her avoid minimizing the abuse and examining the reality.

### 3. Potential for Further Abuse

QUESTIONS: **Is she still living with him? Does he show remorse after the abuse? Has he tried to get help for his abusive behaviour? Does he blame her or some other external pressure for the violence? Does he make promises and fail to keep them? What does she think will make him stop being violent? How fearful is she? How much does he intimidate her?**

PURPOSES:

o to help her realistically assess the potential for further abuse.

o to assist her to explore safety issues for herself and her children.

o to assist her to view her partner's readiness to change in a realistic light.

o to help her get in touch with the degree of fear and intimidation she feels.

### 4. Her Degree of Isolation

QUESTIONS: **Does she have friends and family that she has regular contact with? Do they know about the violence? What is their reaction to the violence? Do their attitudes help her or hinder her? Who can she rely on when she is in need? Does she have a job? Do her co-workers know about the violence? Is her job a source of satisfaction? Is she absent from work as a result of the abuse? Is her job in jeopardy?**

PURPOSES:

o to find out the kind of support system she has access to.

o to assess the quality of her relationships.

o to assess her dependence on her primary relationship.

The more isolated a woman is in her personal and work life, the more dependent she will be on her primary relationship. The more dependent she is on her partner, the less able she will be to take protective action. In essence, the greater her isolation, the more vulnerable she is to remaining in a violent relationship.

### 5. Her Understanding of the Violence

QUESTIONS: **Why does she think he hits her? What is her opinion based on? Does she rationalize the violence? What are her rationalizations? Does she think the violence is justified? Why does she think this? Does she think she can** control her husband's violence?  How has she tried to do this?  Has it been effective in stopping the violence?  How long has it worked?  Does she think violence is a normal response to stress?  Was violence part of her childhood experience?  Has this affected her view of violence as an adult?  Does she believe she must tolerate violence?  If so, how much violence is she willing to tolerate in her life?  What choices does she think are available to her?

PURPOSES:

o      to help her discover what she thinks causes the violence.

o      to help her examine the effectiveness of these beliefs.

o      to help her see if her own beliefs contribute to her position of victim.

6.    Her Coping Responses to the Abuse

QUESTIONS: What does she do during and immediately after a beating?  How has she tried to change her situation?  Have these attempts been successful at stopping the violence?  How does she cope with the stress?  Who has she contacted for help?  Were their responses helpful?  Has she ever left before?  Is she familiar with any self-protective techniques?

PURPOSES:

o      to assess how adaptive her coping responses are.

o      to help her begin to realize the futility in trying to stop his violence.

o      to increase her awareness of protective measures.

---

### EXAMPLES OF:

| Healthy Coping Responses | Unhealthy Coping Responses |
| --- | --- |
| leaving temporarily | drinking to escape the pain |
| o | o |
| calling the police | withdrawing more into herself |
| o | o |
| telling a friend | covering up the abuse |
| o | and pretending it never happened |
| laying an assault charge | o |
| o | blaming herself for the abuse |
| holding him responsible | o |
| for the abuse | taking her rage out |
| o | on the children |
| seeking help | o |
| | attempting suicide |

## 7. Her Rationale for Remaining

QUESTIONS: **What are her reasons for remaining in the abusive relationship? Does she think she can change him? Does she think she can control the violence? Does she want to leave him but has nowhere to go? Is she fearful he will find her and punish her if she leaves? Does she think he needs her? Does she love him? What is her definition of love? Does she believe it's her duty as a wife to remain? Does she stay for religious reasons? Would she leave if she had a way of supporting herself and her children? Does she stay for the sake of the children?**

PURPOSES:

o    to identify her primary reasons for remaining in an unchanged situation.

o    to identify psychological factors, such as "he needs me"; "I'm afraid of him."

o    to identify societal factors, such as "I must stay for the children's sake"; "I can't leave because of my religion."

o    to identify lack of community resources.

## 8. Her Strengths and Weaknesses

QUESTIONS: **What does she see as her strengths? Is she able to identify some good things about herself? Does she have a realistic view of herself? What does she see as her weaknesses? What would she like to change about herself? What does her partner say about her? Does she believe his assessment of her?**

PURPOSES:

o    to help her develop a realistic picture of herself.

o    to help her identify the things in herself she would like to change.

o    to help her separate out her opinion of herself and her partner's opinion of her.

o    to help her develop a positive self-image.

o    to help you redefine her perceived weaknesses into strengths. For example, "you mean to tell me that living under those horrendous circumstances, you were still able to work, raise the children, and keep your home clean."

## 9. Future of the Relationship

QUESTIONS: **What is her relationship like, apart from the violence? What are some of her partner's good qualities? Does she want to continue living with him even if he doesn't change? Does she want to stay with him only if the violence ends? If she separates, will she want the children to have contact with their father? What is their relationship like with her? With their father? Does she** think he is a good father?  What does she base her opinion on?  What are her fears about the future?  What are her worries about herself, her partner and her children?

PURPOSES:

o    to help her clarify her goals.

o    to help her form a plan of action.

o    to help make decisions about the quality of her life and the the quality of her children's future.

o    to help her imagine her future if she remains in the relationship.

o    to help her imagine her future if she leaves the relationship.

10.    Response to Your Intervention

QUESTIONS: **What does she think of you?  What does she think your opinion is of her?  What does she expect you to do?  What does she hope to get from her contact with you?  How does she feel about herself after telling you her story?  What kind of response has she had from her past helpers?**

PURPOSES:

o    to assess her thoughts and feelings about being a client.

o    to help her clarify her expectations.

o    to provide you with the opportunity to dispel myths about counselling, and to set realistic expectations.

o    to allow her to express her frustrations about unhelpful service she may have received in the past and identify fears she may have about the present service being offered.

**Short-Term Intervention with Assaulted Women**

Short-term counselling is sufficient to help **most** assaulted women make the desired and necessary changes in their lives.  A combination of individual and group sessions is most effective in facilitating her change.  The goals of your intervention should be to assist the assaulted woman to:

1.    **choose to no longer be a victim of violence.**

2.    **accept responsibility for improving the quality of her own life.**

These goals should be clearly articulated to her and, at some point, she has to agree with them.  It may take some time for her to understand their significance and this process then becomes part of the counselling.  At no time should she be hurried.  Her individual timing must be respected.

Short-term counselling typically goes through three phases.  These are the initial, middle and ending phases.

I.    Initial Phase

In this phase, which consists of one to six individual sessions, you will be establishing your credibility with her.  It is essential to establish rapport with her and enlist her in a mutual search for answers to her problems.  From your assessment you will now have a fairly clear picture of her unique situation, her rationale for being there, her coping skills, her strengths and weaknesses and her plans for the future.

What you find out in the assessment phase* will lead you to your plan of intervention.  It may be helpful to organize her reasons for remaining in an unchanged situation.  Different reasons require different strategies.

Three examples from my own caseload are given to demonstrate why it is essential to understand a woman's rationale for staying in an unchanged situation before an intervention strategy can be planned.

**The first case is an example of how societal pressures can influence a woman's decision to remain in an unchanged situation.**

**Case Example:**  Kate met her husband when they were both students in medical school.  Their friends and family thought they were "made for each other."  So did they.  They seemed to share the same values and goals for the future.  Tom liked strong, independent women.  They were married shortly after graduation and made plans to set up their medical practice together.  Kate wanted to get established in her career before she had children.

The next five years were described as happy.  They worked side by side building for their future.  Kate got pregnant, a bit sooner than planned, and life changed.  Tom grew moody and resentful of her growing attachment to their baby.  Problems in the latter part of her pregnancy forced her to leave her work prematurely.  Kate depended more on Tom now than at any other point in their relationship.  Their marriage changed.  He began to treat her differently.  The first incident of violence occurred while she was in her ninth month.  She didn't think to leave him.  Instead, she discussed it with her doctor, (a family friend) and he agreed with her that Tom's violent outburst was caused by stress.  Her doctor friend advised, "Try giving him a little extra attention.  He's probably feeling neglected these days."

The baby arrived and Tom never struck her again until the next pregnancy.  Kate felt trapped.  Her friends and family still thought they were

---

*    The assessment phase has been artificially separated from the initial phase for training purposes.  In reality, they occur simultaneously.

the perfect couple. She felt no one would believe her. Tom was such a "nice guy." The situation worsened and Kate was forced to take the children and run. Tom's desperate pleas for forgiveness, combined with pressure from his family, created a great deal of ambivalence in Kate.

She called for help, not knowing whether to give Tom one more chance. She felt guilty, and pressure from family and friends to return made her dilemma even worse. I urged Kate to join the support group for assaulted women and for the first time she admitted the seriousness of her situation.

**Strategy:** What Kate needed was the opportunity to meet other women in the same position, to be believed and supported, and to learn about the reality of violence. The group experience helped her to reaffirm **her** choice to no longer be a victim of violence.

**The following is an example of how a lack of resources can influence a woman's decision to remain in an unchanged situation.**

**Case Example:** Sabra, a young immigrant woman with three small children, lives in daily fear of her husband's beatings. She was completely isolated in her apartment all day. Sabra had no friends and her only outings were with her husband or with his family. She saw no escape from this prison.

Somehow, the police arrived at her home in the midst of one of her husband's violent episodes. They accompanied her and her children to the local shelter. Sabra never looked back.

**Strategy:** All Sabra needed was a safe place to go to, food for herself and her children and money to get herself re-established in a life of her own, to make **her** decision to no longer be a victim of violence.

**The following is an example of how the psychological experiences of the victim can influence her decision to remain in an unchanged situation.**

**Case Example:** Nora, a middle-aged woman, stays with her alcoholic husband despite his periodic violent outbursts. She is used to them. Her father used to drink and abuse her mother as well. Not only that (she's never told a soul), but her Dad used to sexually abuse her from the age of ten until she left home at sixteen. Nora was so glad to meet her husband. He seemed kind and he appeared to really love her. She was not used to getting much praise in her life. She married him thinking she was the luckiest woman alive. When he began to beat her she was devastated. Nora convinced herself that she must have done something wrong to deserve such poor treatment. This view was constantly reinforced by statements from her husband, such as, "If only you would do what you're told, I wouldn't have to hit you." She tried to be a better wife. The violence got worse and more frequent. A friend persuaded her to speak to a counsellor. She was terrified her husband would find out but she came to see me anyway. This was a tremendous step for her.

**Strategy:** Nora needed long-term support and counselling to help her undo the effects of chronic abuse. Her self-esteem was battered as well as her body. Meeting other women in the support group helped but it wasn't enough. She needed individual time and attention from a counsellor who would help **her** begin to choose to no longer be a victim of violence.

These three examples are somewhat simplified to demonstrate the importance of understanding each individual woman's dilemma. Not all assaulted women are the same. They may need different forms of assistance at different times. It is the responsibility of the worker to ensure they get what they need.

## II. Middle Phase

A ten-week group program -- the middle phase of short-term counselling -- is discussed in depth in Chapter 7, Support Groups For Assaulted Women.

## III. Ending Phase

This phase permits you to assess the effectiveness of your intervention thus far. In one to three individual sessions, you can help your client to solidify the changes she has made in both her attitudes and her behaviours. It provides an opportunity for both of you to review her progress, evaluate her changes and set goals for her future.

## SUMMARY OF SHORT-TERM COUNSELLING ISSUES

1.   Dealing with her safety and ongoing protection issues.  (See examples in Appendix E.)

2.   Broadening her support system/decreasing her isolation.

3.   Dealing realistically with her fear by providing her with accurate information, facilitating her access to needed resources and outlining her alternatives.

4.   Increasing her awareness of her rights and responsibilities, such as legal rights.

5.   Helping her understand the impact of violence on her children.

6.   Educating her on the characteristics of the offender so she will be better informed about the dynamics of violence.  This will enable her to clearly separate out his responsibilities (such as control his violent behaviour) and her responsibilities (such as protecting herself).

7.   Mobilizing her anger in a constructive, energy-producing way.

8.   Increasing her sense of control over her environment.

9.   Changing any of her beliefs that may contribute to her victimization such as staying for the sake of the children.

10.  Increasing her economic independence by exploring her opportunities for advancement, such as job re-training.

11.  Dealing with her movement from the victim position to that of personal empowerment.  The transition period is often painful. It brings with it a number of feelings to sort out, such as anger, ambivalence, guilt, sadness.  It may also bring a number of concrete changes that are stressful, such as locating housing and day care, returning to the workforce, coping as a single parent, loss in standard of living.

## Long-Term Intervention with Assaulted Women

The majority of assaulted women do **not** require long-term intervention (loosely defined as ongoing intervention for a period longer than three to four months) to change their situation. Those women most likely to benefit from long-term intervention are:

1. Women who have been abused as children in their family of origin.

2. Women who have witnessed their fathers beating their mothers while they were growing up.

3. Women who have been abused in their marriages for a long period of time (more than twenty years).

4. Women who have become chemically dependent as a means of coping with intolerable living conditions.

5. Women who have completed the group program and are intrigued by the personal growth issues that were raised. They do not **need** the therapy but **want** to pursue further work as a means of enriching their lives. In these cases, the violence issue has usually been resolved.

## Long-Term Counselling Issues

The timing of the transformation from **victim to victor** will vary for individual women. My last support group for assaulted women described their transition well when they referred to themselves as "Victors Over Violence." Briefly described, an assaulted woman starts in the victim position.* Feelings associated with this position include fear, minimization, isolation, depression, helplessness and internalized blame. Effective counselling should help her move to a more independent life position. She moves through many stages, including anger, ambivalence and mourning before she develops a sense of self-worth, an ability to be assertive and a renewed sense of trust in her judgement. Each woman must go through these stages to reach successful resolution of her victimization.

Resolution of **ambivalence** requires practice, a great deal of practice. A woman needs the experience of repeated success to overcome her learned helplessness. She will go back and forth living out both sides until either the offender makes solid, lasting changes or until she realizes she is no longer willing to tolerate the situation. The bad must far outweigh the good in her cost-benefit analysis.

---

\*    The dependency cycle, which reflects these life positions, is described in detail by Susan Harris in Chapter 7.

The **turning point** for many women occurs when she is able to realize that no matter what she does, she cannot control her husband's behaviour. She recognizes the violence is not her fault.

**Planned separations** are preferable to **forced separations.** Women who are forced to leave their home prematurely (e.g., those who flee for safety reasons) will often return to resolve the ambivalence. Women who leave successfully, thereby ending their victimization, are likely women who have sorted out a plan of action and are able to follow it through at their own pace.

Reluctant leavers most often return. These are usually the women in crisis accommodation. Given this reality, the goal should be to arm them with survival techniques so that the next time they are in danger they will be better equipped to protect themselves.

Ideally, a woman should be helped to weigh the advantages and disadvantages of remaining in her situation **before** the next crisis occurs. Her thinking will be more reliable and less emotionally wrenching to her and her children. A forced departure means instant change, which is far more difficult to cope with.

It is imperative that counsellors not **measure success** by whether or not a woman leaves her situation permanently. Often a worker pushes a woman to make changes before she is ready. A worker may feel angry and be tempted to blame her or avoid her if she decides to stay or return to her partner. **It is more realistic and more effective to measure success by the woman's increased ability to protect herself.**

Emphasis on her staying or leaving heightens her internal conflict and makes her feel worse about herself. If you believe your role is to increase her positive feelings about herself, you must foster her ability to make choices in her life. This is the difference between empowering her and rescuing her. Do not let your anxiety interfere with her safety. Pressure sends her backward not forward. **The goal is to help her choose to no longer be a victim of violence.**

The victim often feels conflict because she feels she **still loves her husband.** What is love? How does she love him? Is it addictive, freeing, romantic or sexual? Get her to explore and analyze her feelings. Too often, we accept pat statements about such things as love without fully understanding their meaning and their hold on a person.

A small number of women, damaged by a lifetime of abuse, may **think** they need the excitement and intensity the violent man brings with him. The unpredictable nature of the relationship and the insecurity of the relationship keeps her on her toes -- dancing. She has no time to rest, no respite from the intensity of feeling. It is sometimes described as a "love addiction," where a woman will get a rush from the highs in the relationship and will experience despair (similar to withdrawal symptoms) in the lows of the relationship. This kind of relationship allows her to avoid dealing with her own depression and emptiness. This woman is particularly vulnerable to being labelled masochistic. Even if **she** thinks she is masochistic, it is essential that the counsellor not be misled. She is hooked on the highs (the good times in the relationship) **not** the lows (the bad times when violence is likely). Successful resolution requires a joint effort between the counsellor and the client to patiently unravel her history of victimization and examine its impact on her life.

Those women most vulnerable to considering **violence as a norm** are usually the street-smart women who have had a long history of abuse and have so toughened themselves to deal with a hostile world that are unable to accept genuine tenderness without suspicion. They think, "he must be after something." They have developed an ability to cope with and expect a certain amount of violence in their lives. However, even these women have their limits. Find out what they are and work to change them. Recognize the differences in women's lives and respect their individual timing for change. Successful resolution requires **unlearning** years of messages that uphold self-destructive beliefs. It requires patience and fortitude on the part of both the counsellor and the client.

The assaulted woman needs time to **grieve her losses** -- loss of her innocence, loss of the good parts of her relationship, loss of her marital status, loss of her lifestyle, loss of her hope that things will work out.

The assaulted woman must **resolve the anger and guilt** she feels towards her partner and herself. The assaulted woman often has a great deal of stored-up rage towards her partner. For years she has had to hide her anger and swallow her fury. She needs time and permission to express openly her hostilities towards him. She needs to be assured that it is rational to feel the way she does, given the abuse she has been forced to tolerate from him. The longer and more severe the abuse was, the greater her anger will be towards her partner. It is important not to dissuade her from her anger prematurely. She needs time to ventilate!

She often feels both anger and guilt towards herself as well as her partner. She needs time to forgive herself for choosing him as a partner. Even though she may not have known of his violence, she berates herself for not picking up some of the signals she now realizes were there, such as his temper tantrums. She needs time to understand and accept her reasons for tolerating the abuse and then, after accepting them as legitimate reasons, she needs to forgive herself. She needs to come to terms with her guilt about how she exposed her children to her victim role-modelling and that in combination with their father's violent role-modelling, the children may now have serious problems. The longer the woman stayed in a violent relationship, the greater the guilt, especially if she believed her staying was in the best interests of her children. It is important for the counsellor to redirect some of her client's anger at the proper target: the real problem is a society that teaches that "any father is better than no father," "a woman without a man is nothing" and "women should stay for the sake of the kids." The counselling experience should begin a process of consciousness-raising.

Many assaulted women have coped with their situation by burying their **sexual needs and feelings.** For women, generally, their own sexual satisfaction has often been given only secondary importance to that of their partners. Women may have grown to hate their bodies, especially if they have been badly abused sexually. Self-hatred leads to many self-destructive habits, such as poor nutritional habits, eating disturbances, obesity, chemical dependence and suicidal thoughts and actions.

Assaulted women will benefit from **assertiveness training.** They need not only to define their needs but also to take responsibility for getting their needs met. Their fear of retaliation has prevented them from standing up for themselves. They need to be encouraged to defend their rights.

Assaulted women struggle with conflicting feelings of **independence versus dependence.** They need to recognize the difference between healthy and unhealthy dependence. Ultimately, they must come to terms with balancing their need for intimacy with the need to be their own person.

An assaulted woman with children may need to redefine her **parenting role.** She may need to develop an increased awareness of her children's needs, to learn new ways of communicating with them, to examine her methods of discipline and her ways of expressing her love. Her children may be her only source of joy or they may be a constant reminder of her failure as a mother. She needs to understand how violence has impacted on her life as well as on her children's lives. Her children may experience her as a passive, compliant person with little authority or control. They may identify with their father's aggression and even take on some of his abusive behaviours. It is not unusual for children from wife-assault homes to show disrespect, hostility and even outright violence towards their mother. If she has a history of child abuse in her own family-of-origin, she may also be vulnerable to behaving violently herself. One study suggests 35% of assaulted women have grown up in a violent home.[3]  She will need a great deal of support and guidance to break the cycle of abuse.  A parenting support group in conjunction with a children's group is an effective method of breaking this cycle (Refer to Chapter 9).

Whether separated or not, **her future relationship with the offender** will have changed.  Does she want to have contact with him and in what way?

Finally, an assaulted woman must sort out her **future relationship with men.**  She must be able to define her needs and discover her likes and dislikes in relation to men.  Is she able to recognize societal messages that have contributed to her victimization?  The counsellor must help her trust her feelings and help her pay attention to any potential pitfalls (e.g., male chauvinism, jealousy, hot temper).

## Suggested Reading -- Working with Women

Conroy, Kathryn.  "Long-term Treatment Issues With Battered Women," in The Many Faces of Family Violence.  S. Flanzer (ed.).  Springfield, Illinois:  Charles C. Thomas 1982, pp. 24 - 33.

Fleming, Jennifer.  Stopping Wife Abuse.  Garden City, New York:  Anchor Books, 1979.

Fortune, Rev. Marie, and Hormann, Denise.  Family Violence:  A Workshop Manual for Clergy and Other Service Providers.  Rockville, Maryland:  National Clearing House in Domestic Violence, April 1981.

Gornick, Vivian, and Noran, Barbara (eds.).  Women in Sexist Society:  Studies in Power and Powerlessness.  New York:  Basic Books, 1971.

Lefeuvre, Joan.  Fresh Start . . . Is This Book For You?  Ontario:  Peterborough YWCA, 1982.  Available from:  YWCA of Canada, Resource Centre, 80 Gerrard Street East,  Toronto, Ontario M5B 1G6.  Tel: (416) 593-9886.

Levine, Helen.  Feminist Counselling.  Reprint available from Education Wife Assault, 427 Bloor Street West, Toronto, Ontario M5S 1X7.

Lichtenstein,  Doreen, Waisberg, Barbara and Small, Shirley Endicott.  A

---

[3]  Roy, Maria (ed.).  Ibid.

Program To Train Lay Counsellors -- To Counsel and Support Battered Women. Toronto: Education Wife Assault, 1984.

Manual for Crisis Intervention. NOW Domestic Violence Project, Inc., 1917 Washtenaw Avenue, Ann Arbour, Michigan 48104. Tel: (313) 995-5444, 995-5460.

Matsakis-Scarato, Aphrodite. "Counselling Battered Women." Reprint available from: Education Wife Assault, 427 Bloor Street West, Toronto, Ontario M5S 1X7.

NiCarthy, Ginny. Getting Free: A Handbook for Women in Abusive Relationships. Washington: Seal Press, 1982.

NiCarthy, Ginny, Merriam, Karen, and Coffman, Sandra. Talking It Out: A Guide To Groups For Abused Women. Washington: Seal Press, 1984.

Ruitort, Monica, and Small, Shirley Endicott. Working with Assaulted Immigrant Women: A Handbook for Lay Counsellors. Toronto: Education Wife Assault, 1984.

Small, Shirley, and Greenlee, Carol. Wife Abuse -- Understanding The Issues: A Workshop Manual for Community Groups. Available from Education Wife Assault, Toronto, 1985.

Walker, Lenore. The Battered Woman. New York: Harper and Row, 1979.

Wilcoxen, Marilyn. Assaulted Women: A Handbook for Health Professionals. Toronto: Education Wife Assault, 1982.

Women's Counselling, Referral and Education Centre (WCREC). Helping Ourselves -- A Handbook For Women Starting Groups. Toronto: 1984.

Wright, Joan. Chemical Dependency and Violence: Working With Dually Affected Families: A Cross-Training Program Manual for Counsellors and Advocates. Available from: Wisconsin Clearinghouse, 1954 East Washington Avenue, Madison, WI 53704.

Wyckoff, Hogie. Solving Problems Together. New York: Grove Press, 1980.

## 5   COUNSELLING THE VIOLENT MAN

Before helping men who assault their wives, counsellors must hold the following values and beliefs, which have been adapted for the purpose of this manual.[1]

1.     The offender is solely responsible for his own violence and abuse.  No matter how much stress there is in a relationship, the offender is not provoked to use violence.  He chooses violence as a means of coping with stress.  The victim cannot cause or eliminate the offender's violence.

2.     Once the offender uses violence to cope with stress, he will rarely spontaneously stop using violence.  Violence is a behaviour that is addictive and immediately effective, even though destructive in the long run.

3.     Violence is learned by individuals through the culture.  The dominant culture teaches that people who are in authority or are "right" can control or manipulate other people.  For example:  parents can "discipline" or hit a child for not thinking or behaving the "right" way.

4.     **Couple or family counselling with the offender present should never happen until violence has stopped, and the victim is no longer afraid of the offender.**  It is too dangerous to discuss the problems of the family until all members are safe from being abused.  Any problems with communication cannot realistically be addressed while one is blatantly abusing power or force.  To develop trust, equal communication, and the mutual support necessary for solving family problems, safety must first be achieved.

5.     Group counselling is much more effective than individual counselling. Groups lessen the shame, guilt and isolation felt by each offender by demonstrating the commonality of abuse.  Because group members are at different stages in their efforts towards nonviolent behaviours, they have more opportunity to teach and practice skills already learned, or learn from positive role models.

6.     Group leaders must be aware of their own attitudes and experiences with violence.  The group leaders provide information and positive role models, and confront violent values and behaviours.  The group leaders should be sensitive to the overt and subtle destructiveness of all violence.

---

[1]     Adapted from Barbara Pressman, Ibid.

7.     Unlike assaulted women, men who assault their wives benefit from contact with both male and female counsellors. This provides them the opportunity to have alternative role models. It is particularly important for them to witness male counsellors who are willing to take a stand against violence against women and who are comfortable with expressing their thoughts and feelings. Also, it is important that they have female counsellors who model strong assertive behaviours and who are not intimidated by violent behaviour.

**Intervening with the Violent Man:     The First Contact**

There may be a number of reasons that prompt the violent man to reach out for help. Some of these are:

1.     His wife has threatened to leave him if he does not get some help.

2.     His wife has already left him and is refusing to return until he gets help.

3.     He has been advised or ordered by the courts to seek counselling for his violent behaviour.

4.     He has heard about a group program (e.g., through a newspaper article) for men like himself and he wants to get more information about it.

5.     He may be seeking help for some other problem, such as physical symptoms, depression, problems at work, alcohol or drug abuse.

Most violent men are under some kind of duress when they call you. Seldom do they seek help voluntarily. This is primarily because they do **not** realize they are responsible for their problems when they first contact you. Remember that one of their characteristics is externalization of blame.

There are three primary tasks at the first stage of intervention. They are:

1.     To ensure the safety of the assaulted woman.

2.     To ensure the safety of the violent man.

3.     To engage the violent man in the counselling process.

As in the previous chapter, here are some questions designed to help ascertain the extent of the problem.

1.     Your first task is to assess the safety of the assaulted woman.

QUESTIONS: **Where is she?  Where are the children?  Are they safe?  Has he just abused them?  Are they injured?  Is he about to abuse them?  Ask to speak to the assaulted woman or to get the phone number of where she can be reached.**

PURPOSES:

o    to ensure the assaulted woman's and the children's safety.

o    to assure the violent man that you take his violence seriously.

o    to assess his immediate potential for violence.

2.    <u>The next task is to assure the safety of the violent man.</u>

QUESTIONS: **What is his present emotional state?  Is he depressed, anxious, enraged?  Is he suicidal?  Has he ever attempted suicide in the past?  Is he on drugs or drinking?**

PURPOSES:

o    to assess the likelihood of suicidal behaviour.

o    to assess the need for immediate addiction intervention.

o    to assess the need for immediate psychiatric intervention.

o    to assure the offender that you are genuinely concerned for his personal safety as well as his family's.

**IMPORTANT:**    If you think he is likely to be dangerous to himself, to his wife, to the children or to anyone, intervene immediately.  Take his threats seriously! CALL THE POLICE.

3.    <u>Once you establish the safety of the family, your next task is to engage the violent man in the counselling process.</u>

o    Establish some rapport with him.  Try to find the part of him in pain and speak to that.

o    Establish your credibility with him.  Let him know of your experience in this area and your belief that this problem can be solved.

o    Clarify your role.  Let him know clearly what he can expect of you.  For example, you **can** help him stop his violent behaviour, you **cannot** get his wife back for him.

o    Affirm his ability to change.  He is not crazy nor is he a monster. Violence is learned.  He can unlearn it.

o    Help him explore alternatives to his abusive behaviour.  For example, he could talk to a friend or call a distress line.

o    Help him begin to identify the consequences of his abusive behaviour, such as criminal charges, possibility of causing permanent injury or death, placing his relationship in jeopardy.

o    Let him know what resources are available to assist him in his changes. For example, addiction counselling, group programs for offenders, individual counselling.

o    Offer to make him an immediate referral if you are unable to see him yourself, or if there is a better resource available, such as a men's support group.

o    Encourage him to consider a temporary separation until he is sure he will not endanger his wife or children.

o    If his wife has already left and you know her whereabouts, you cannot tell him where she is but you can assure him of her safety and that his children are being well taken care of.

o    If his wife has left, help him understand why she had to do that. For example, she was scared of him and had to leave for safety reasons. Try to enlist his cooperation in the separation.

o    Establish ongoing contact.

**Tips for the Counsellor**

1.    If you know he has been violent because his wife, the police or a shelter worker have told you so, do **not** ask him if has been. He might be tempted to lie to you and later be humiliated when you confront him with the truth.

2.    Speak to him in a calm, matter-of-fact manner without judging him. Your goal is to help **change** his violent behaviour, not to make him feel worse about himself. His self-image is shaky enough.

3.    If you feel angry at what he's done (a normal reaction), reserve it for another time and place. Unlike your contact with the victim, where your anger can be a validating and mobilizing force for her, it serves no useful purpose in your contact with him. It escalates his anxieties and increases his defenses. If he senses you are attacking him or judging him, you have no hope of engaging him. His reaction to your anger can also endanger his partner's safety if he becomes more enraged.

4.    Do **not** let him intimidate you. Even if you are intimidated, do not show it. His intimidation tactics are based on fear and are a desperate attempt to gain control of the situation. Let him know you are aware of what he's doing but it won't work. Once he knows he cannot intimidate you, he often expresses relief at being seen clearly and still accepted. For example, "I felt a lot better once I realized you could see through me and that I couldn't scare you off. I don't like being this way, I just don't know how else to be."

5.    Some counsellors fear a direct approach will offend him and he will leave counselling. This is a possibility for some men and means that legal consequences -- laying an assault charge or court-mandated treatment --may be more effective in facilitating his change. For most men who have contact with a counsellor, the direct, non-judgemental approach is effective. Remember, **to**

**avoid confronting the violence is to deal with him under false pretences.** Eventually, he will leave counselling because he knows you are either afraid, unwilling or unable to deal with the real problem, his abusive behaviour.

6.    Legal interventions, such as restraining orders and peace bonds, can be quite effective if he is respectful of the law.  If he has a criminal record or is violent outside of the home, this suggests he is **not** respectful of the law.

7.    In those cases where a separation is desirable for the safety of the victim, attempt to gain his cooperation for a separation plan.  It will be more successful if he agrees to it.  If a separation cannot occur, then an immediate alternative might be to have a third person, such as a supportive father-in-law, move in with the family temporarily.  This is not a long-term solution, only a temporary protective measure.  Both spouses need support throughout the process.  Even if they do not stay married, successful resolution of the crisis protects her and deters him from continuing to abuse women in future relationships.

8.    Emotional support must be given to both spouses through the separation process.  If you cannot work with the offender, link him up to a supportive resource such as clergy, informed friends or family or a community police officer.  This is a temporary measure until an appropriate resource can be found.  He should not be left alone.

9.    The worker must see the offender's strengths as well as the offender's weaknesses.

o    If your abhorrence of the violence interferes with your acceptance of his personhood (this does **not** mean condoning his violence) then you will alienate him.  He will sense you despise him and thus will be forced to further defend himself.

o    Failure to see his good qualities means running the risk of alienating the victim.  You may persecute her and blame her for being ambivalent about the relationship (especially if **you** have decided she should leave him).

o    A negative view of the offender also means you will have difficulty truly empathizing with her genuine concern for her partner.

o    **Even if you do not think it's your responsibility to work with the violent man, you owe it to the assaulted woman to understand his issues clearly so you can effectively help her.**

10.    Some counsellors focus only on his strengths, believing that if his self-esteem increases, his violent behaviour will subside.  **This is not true.**  In fact, if his violence is minimized or ignored, his anxiety escalates, thus increasing the chance of violence.  He knows you are not seeing him clearly.  He comes to

believe that you are just one more person he is able to charm and con. This does not create a basis of genuine trust on which to build. Eventually he will drop out of counselling!

**Assessment Interview with the Violent Man**

Once you have dealt with the initial crisis -- assuring the safety of both the victim and the offender -- you can begin the assessment phase of the counselling process. In reality, the two are inseparable. Evaluation of your intervention and safety checks are an ongoing part of every contact with the offender. As with the victim, the questions posed during your initial interviews are in fact part of your intervention. The questions must be purposeful and therapeutic in nature. Attention must be paid to both verbal and non-verbal responses and these responses will guide you in your development of an intervention plan tailored to the offender's unique needs.

1.   Family of Origin

QUESTIONS: **Would he describe his childhood as happy, sad, secure? Did he like himself? What were his relationships like with his mother, father, sisters, brothers? What form of discipline was used? How was affection shown? Was there any abuse in the family? Who was the victim? Who was the offender? Was he sexually abused as a child? By whom? Did he ever sexually abuse someone else, such as his sister? When did he leave home and under what circumstance? What were his expectations about relationships with women? Relationships with men? Were there special factors that influenced his life -- religious, cultural, geographic factors? What were his expectations of his future regarding money, family, career, education?**

PURPOSES:
o      to help him connect his childhood experience with his experience as as adult.

o      to help him use his own victimization as a child to empathize with his partner's experience as a victim.

o      to help him uncover the influences in his past life that form the foundation of his present values and beliefs.

2.   History of Violence
QUESTIONS: **What does he define as abuse? When did he first behave violently? Was he violent in any of his past relationships? Ask for details. Is he violent outside of his present relationship? Ask for details. Does he abuse the children? Have him describe, in detail, the last three incidents of violence in his present relationship. What made him angry? What were the triggers?**

What did he do?  How did he stop himself?  What did he do afterwards?  What was the impact on him?  On his partner?  On his children?  What was the worst episode?  What is his understanding of why the violence occurs?

PURPOSES:
o      to help him acknowledge his abusive behaviour.

o      to help him articulate his own rationalizations for the violence.

o      to help identify his pattern of violence.

o      to help him identify the consequences of his behaviour.

o      to help him begin to see that his behaviour is within his own control.

3.      Presence of Alcohol or Drugs/General Health

QUESTIONS: Is he presently drinking or on drugs?  Does he have a history of alcohol or drug abuse?  Does he behave differently when he is under the influence of alcohol or drugs?  Has he ever tried to stop drinking or taking drugs?  How?  Did he have any withdrawal symptoms?  Have him describe them.  Has he had a recent medical check-up?  Is he generally in good health?

PURPOSES:
o      to assess his degree of addictive behaviour.

o      to discover the relationship between his violence and his abuse of drugs/alcohol.
o      to assess his general health.

Note:   If the violent man is addicted to drugs or alcohol, this must be dealt with prior to or in conjunction with his participation in a counselling program.  If there is any doubt about his intellectual or neurological functioning, testing should be done.  A complete medical check-up is also a helpful tool in addressing his needs in an holistic way.

4.      Publicity of the Violence

QUESTIONS: Who knows about the violence?  How have they reacted to it?  Do they hold him responsible?  Do they blame his partner?  Do they make excuses for him?  Do the responses he receives help him change or keep him from changing?

PURPOSES:
o      to examine the messages he receives from his family and peers.

o      to increase his awareness about those factors that help or hinder his ability to change.

Note:   The more public his violence is, the greater the chance he stands of receiving useful messages from his peers, family and community at large.  The more pressure placed on him to curb his violent behaviour, the more likely it will stop.

5. <u>Degree of Isolation</u>

QUESTIONS: **Does he have friends or family that he has regular contact with? How do they react to him? Who can he turn to when he's in need? Does he have a job? How does his violence affect his work? Do his colleagues at work know about his violence?**

PURPOSES:
o       to find out the kind of support system he has access to.

o       to assess the quality of his relationships.

o       to assess his dependence on the primary relationship.

**Note:**   The more isolated a man is in his personal and work life, the more dependent he will be on his primary relationship.  The more dependent he is on his partner, the more devastated and threatened he will be by any act of independence on her part.  In essence, the greater the isolation, the greater the possibility of his being dangerous.

6.    <u>Primary Relationship</u>

QUESTIONS: **How does he view his relationship?  How does he feel about his wife?  How does he think she feels about him?  Is she fearful of him?  Is she intimidated by him?  Is he able to articulate her needs separate from his own? Is she suicidal?  Is she depressed?  Is he intimidated by her?  What are the positives in their relationship?  What are the negatives?  Has he ever considered a separation?**

PURPOSES:
o       to help him begin to empathize with her feelings.

o       to help him separate his feelings from his partner's.

o       to help him examine the impact of violence on his partner and the relationship as a whole.

o       to help him realize the alternatives to a poor relationship,such as separation, counselling.

7.    <u>Relationship With His Children</u>

QUESTIONS: **Have him describe his involvement with his children.   How attached is he to the children?  Is he concerned with their welfare?  How is his concern demonstrated?  Does he realize the impact of his violent behaviour on them?  Is he able to articulate their needs separate from his own?  Does he abuse them —psychologically, physically, sexually?  Are they fearful of him?**

PURPOSES:
o       to assess the quality of his relationship with his children.

o       to assess his ability to parent them.

o    to assess his motives for contacting the children in the event of a separation.

**Note:** Sometimes, after a separation, offenders will use their children as an excuse to continue contact with their wives. Some children may be abused solely as a means of causing pain to their mother.

8.    <u>Motivation to Change</u>

QUESTIONS: **What are his reasons for seeking help?  Does he think there is anything wrong with his behaviour?  Does he want to change his behaviour? What does he see as the benefits of changing?  What will be the cost to him if he does not want to change?  What if his present relationship does not work out?  Is he still wanting to change his violence?  What does he think of you and the help you are offering?**

PURPOSES:

o    to assess his degree of internal motivation.

o    to help him realistically examine his own motives.

o    to help him clarify his expectations about the service being offered.

**Working with the Violent Man Always Includes**
**Ensuring the Assaulted Woman's Safety**

If you are only seeing the violent man, try to arrange for one interview with his partner.  The purpose of this interview is to get an accurate portrayal of the frequency and severity of past violence, the potential for further violence, the degree of fear and intimidation felt by his partner and her goals for the future of the relationship.

If she does not want to be involved in his counselling, she should not be coerced into it, regardless of how desperate the offender is or how willing he is to change.  She has a right to remain on the periphery.  The offender may place a great deal of pressure on the counsellor to act as a go-between.  Be clear about your role.  Only have contact with her to clarify the facts about the violence and to help her maximize her safety.

o    Make sure she has access to needed resources.

o    Inform her about the kind of counselling her partner is receiving.

o    Assure her that any information she shares is confidential.

o    Assure her that if she does have contact with the offender and has concerns about what he tells her (for example, "my counsellor told me I'm cured and we can get back together again") she should feel free to confirm the story with his worker.
    **The worker's first priority is her safety!**

The violent man should **always** know that the worker will contact his partner if the worker thinks she is in danger. **This should be made clear to him at the outset.** For example, "Anything we talk about will be confidential except when I feel you are in danger or your partner is. I will take the necessary steps to ensure your safety and your family's safety."

The violent man is often relieved that someone is taking him seriously and will take charge if necessary. This also avoids any chance of the worker feeling divided over breaching a confidential issue.

## Goals and Issues

### Goals

The goals of your intervention should be to assist the offender to stop his violent behaviour and to accept responsibility for improving the quality of his own life.

After the first contact, group counseling is by far the preferred choice of intervention.* There are three primary reasons to continue seeing him individually:

1. He is not ready, willing or able (e.g., because of shift work) to join a group program yet. Continued individual contact should be focussed on internalizing his responsibility for his behaviour in preparation for a group.

2. There is no group program available or an opening is not immediately available. Individual counselling can be a bridge until a group is available.

3. If the offender is in severe crisis requiring additional support, individual counselling can act as an adjunct to the group program.

### Issues

1. Helping him internalize responsibility for ending violent behaviour.

2. Informing him about the facts of wife assault.

3. Increasing his awareness about personal patterns of violence, such as pre-violence cues.

4. Helping him develop alternatives to violence.

---

\*    Refer to Chapter 8 - Group Model for Men Who Assault Their Partners. If there is not a group available in your community, action should be taken to develop one. Ideally it should be an all male co-leadership team or a male/female co-leadership team. It is helpful if the offender can be exposed to both male and female role models who challenge sexist stereotypes at some point in the counselling process.

5.     Learning, to express anger in constructive ways.

6.     Developing new skills for coping with stress (e.g., relaxation techniques).

7.     Changing his need to control others to need for control of self.

8.     Unlearning destructive myths.

9.     Decreasing social and emotional isolation.

10.    Decreasing dependence on the primary relationship.

11.    Learning to accept differences in partner and children without taking it as a personal rejection.

12.    Developing flexible definitions of male and female roles.

13.    Developing respect for the value of women and children.

14.    Expanding his ability to identify and express a wide range of feelings.

15.    Developing the ability to nurture himself and others. For example, proper diet, proper rest, adequate exercise, absence of self-destructive behaviours.

16.    Developing empathy for his partner and his children.

17.    Improving his parenting skills.

18.    Developing his interpersonal skills.

19.    Developing his personal power through assertiveness training.

20.    Helping him to accept the possibility of his marriage ending.

21.    Increasing sexual awareness -- focusing on the process of loving rather than performing.

22.    Helping him recognize his strengths as well as his weaknesses.

---

### RATIONALE FOR COURT-MANDATED TREATMENT

1.     Most offenders do not come forward voluntarily.

2.     Offenders may drop out of counselling if they feel threatened, if they feel sufficiently calmed in the early stages of intervention or if they realize their wives will not be returning to them or have already returned to them.

3.     Offenders must be externally motivated until they are able to develop some internal motivation (this is part of the intervention).

4.     Offenders must be held accountable for their actions. If there is not sufficient change through the group program (that is, measurable proof of the violence ending), they must be returned to the criminal justice system to face the consequences. Counselling should not be used as a means to avoid legal consequences.

---

## A Comment on Marriage Counselling

Marriage counselling is a viable option only after the following conditions have been met:

1.     the offender has accepted full responsibility for his violent behaviour and has made concerted efforts to change that behaviour.

2.     the victim is clearly able to protect herself, measured by her understanding and willingness to assume responsibility for her protection.

3.     the potential for further abuse is minimal (there is never a guarantee).

4.     the degree of intimidation and fear felt by the victim is significantly reduced, so as to not interfere with open discussion of marital issues. Make sure she does not think the issues she raises during the session will be used as an excuse by her husband to assault her after the session.

5.     the goals of the couple are mutually agreed upon and couple work is entered into freely by both partners. Make sure he has not instructed her to remain silent on contentious issues.

Marriage counselling should emphasize the following:

1.     Differential responsibility for violence and safety/protection. Make sure this includes ending psychological abuse as well as physical abuse. This is often much more difficult to eliminate.

2.     Clear communication.

3.     Conflict resolution and compromise.

4.     Equitable division of labour.

5.     Flexibility in sex roles.

6.     Shared parenting skills.

7.     Mutual sexual satisfaction.

8.     Balance between needs of the primary relationship with their individual needs.

The goal of marriage counselling is psychological interdependence, where both partners not only experience intimacy as they desire but also have the capacity to be separate individuals.

## Suggested Reading -- Working with Men

Browning, Jim. Stopping the Violence: Canadian Programmes for Assaultive Men. Ottawa: National Clearing House on Family Violence, Health and Welfare, 1984.

Currie, David. "A Toronto Model." Social Work With Groups 6 (3/4, Fall/Winter), 1983, pp. 179-188.

Farrell, Warren. The Liberated Man -- Beyond Masculinity: Freeing Men and Their Relationships With Women. New York: Random House, 1974.

Ganley, Anne. Court-Mandated Counselling for Men Who Batter: A Three Day Workshop for Mental Health Professionals. Washington, D.C.: Center for Women Policy Studies, 1982.

Goldberg, Herb. The Hazards of Being Male. New York: Signet, 1976.

Goldberg, Herb. The New Male-Female Relationship. New York: Signet, 1984.

Kiley, Dan. The Peter Pan Syndrome. New York: Avon, 1984.

Purdy, Frances, and Nickle, N. "Practice Principles for Working with Groups of Men Who Batter." Social Work with Groups 4 (3/4, Fall/Winter), 1981, pp. 111-122.

Robbins, Paul. "Must Men Be Friendless?" Leadership. Fall, 1984, pp. 24-29.

Roy, Maria (ed.). The Abusive Partner: An Analysis of Domestic Battering. New York: Van Nostrand Reinhold, 1982.

Sonkin, Daniel, and M. Durphy. Learning to Live Without Violence: A Handbook for Men. San Francisco: Volcano Press, 1982.

Viscott, David. The Language of Feelings. New York: Pocket Books, 1976.

**Suggested Reading For Couples**

Jones, Muriel. <u>Marriage Is For Loving</u>. Menlo Park, California: Addison-Wesley, 1979.

Lasswell, Marcia, and N. Lobseng. <u>No-Fault Marriages</u>. Garden City, New York: Doubleday, 1976.

Rubin, Lillian. <u>Intimate Strangers, Men and Women Together</u>. New York: Harper and Rowe Publishers, 1983.

# 6 ISSUES RELATED TO CHILDREN

Any child who lives with violence or the threat of violence is a child in need of protection, a child at risk.[1] Four possibilities exist:

1.    A man who abuses his wife may also abuse his children.

2.    A woman who is abused may vent her rage and frustration on her children.

3.    Children may be accidently hurt when they try to stop the violence or protect their mother.

4.    Children witnessing wife assault in their home may grow up to be abusive husbands or assaulted wives.

Even if children are not the direct target of violence, by being exposed to violence they suffer from tremendous emotional abuse and possible neglect.

They seldom have an adequate relationship with their fathers. Although many children living with the threat of violence are close to their mothers, the mothers cannot be fully available to tend to the children's needs when they are forced to fight for their own survival on a daily basis. This is not said to fault mothers. Many have done quite incredible jobs of raising their children in the face of horrendous odds. However, the only way to end the generational cycle of abuse is to stop it today.

---

[1]    Fleming, Jennifer. Stopping Wife Abuse. Garden City, New York: Anchor Books, 1979.

Imagine growing up in a home where . . .

| Your Dad | Your Mom |
|---|---|
| o beats your Mom and threatens to kill her | o feels terrified of your Dad |
| o threatens to kill himself | o tries to escape from your Dad's temper |
| o calls your Mom nasty names | o screams out for help |
| o destroys your Mom's precious possessions | o creeps around the house so Dad won't get mad |
| o tries to hurt you or your pet | o picks up the kitchen knife to defend herself |
| o throws things around in a fit of rage | o forgives your Dad when he cries |
| o believes he has a right to hurt your Mom | o thinks she deserves to be hit |
| o believes your Mom deserves to be hit | o makes excuses for your Dad's temper tantrums |
| o tells you not to listen to your Mom because "she's a rotten mother" | o feels helpless to change her life |
| o is angry a good deal of the time | o feels depressed and cries a good deal of time |
| o sometimes cries because he hurts your Mom | o gets furious at your Dad and takes it out on you |
| o says he can't control himself | o is frustrated and yells a lot |
| o walks around like a time-bomb ready to blow up any minute | o promises to leave if your Dad ever hits her again and then she doesn't |
| o promises he will never hurt you or your Mom again and then he does | |

## The Cycle of Violence Continues[2]

It is little wonder children react the way they do. Unless someone actively intervenes, the cycle of violence continues. There is substantial evidence suggesting that offenders have grown up in violent homes -- either being victims of abuse themselves or witnessing their fathers beating their mothers -- leaving little doubt that **violent behaviour is learned.***

Although the majority of wife assault victims have not grown up in violent homes, those that have experience much greater difficulty standing up for themselves and taking protective action leaving little doubt that **victim behaviour is learned.**

Children from violent homes end up believing that

o   it is all right for husbands to hit wives.

o   violence is a way to win arguments.

o   big people have power they often misuse.

o   men are bullies who push women and children around.

o   women are victims and can't take care of themselves or their children.

## The Impact of Violence on Children

When upset, children generally tend to act out their distress rather than talk about it. In a home where fearful silence and tension is the norm, children are even more vulnerable to repressing their feelings. Feelings of fear, anger, guilt, sadness, worry, confusion and ambivalence often get submerged. These reactions surface in other ways. Children know their parents are not able to deal with their hurts or even be aware of them at times. Because their parents are too tied up with their own miseries, children are forced to find indirect

---

*   Not all children in violent homes are doomed to repeat their parents' patterns. Some children are disgusted by their experiences and completely reject the use of violence in their adult lives. One study of offenders found that only 12% of the offenders' siblings chose to be violent in their adulthood. (Russell Dobash and Rebecca Emerson Dobash, Violence Against Wives, New York: Free Press, 1979.) It is crucial that we do not participate in a self-fulfilling prophecy giving children the message that if they grow up in a violent home they will become violent themselves. **Children have choices.** Our job is to make those choices available to them.

[2]   Roy, Maria (ed.). The Abusive Partner: An Analysis of Domestic Battering. New York: Van Nostrand Reinhold, 1980.

ways of expressing their hurts, getting the attention they need. In essence, they are crying out for help.

The following reactions have been observed in children and are separated into groups according to their age and stage of development. Any child could have some of these symptoms, but children from violent homes are more vulnerable to excessive symptoms of stress.

## Preschoolers (birth to 5 years)

o      physical complaints, such as stomach-aches, headaches.

o      sleep disturbances, such as insomnia, heightened fear of the dark, resistance to bedtime.

o      bed-wetting.

o      excessive separation anxieties.

o      whining, clinging, anxiety.

o      failure to thrive.

## School-age children (6 to 12 years)

School-age Children may:

o      become seductive or manipulative as a way of reducing tension in the home.

o      hang around their house a lot believing their presence will control the violence and will protect their Mom -- or they may do the exact opposite, avoiding their home as much as possible believing their absence will improve their parents' relationship.

o      fear being abandoned.

o      fear being killed or fear themselves killing someone else.

o      fear their own anger and others' anger.

o      exhibit eating disturbances, such as overeating, undereating or hoarding food.

o      become insecure and distrustful of their environment, especially if there are frequent unpredictable parental separations that they are not informed about.

The effects of sex-role socialization can be seen as school-age children tend to separate their behaviours along sex lines.

| Girls | Boys |
|---|---|
| o   continuation of somatic complaints. | o   aggressive, acting-out behaviour. |
| o   withdrawn, passive, compliant, clinging behaviour. | o   temper tantrums. |
| o   approval-seeking behaviour. | o   fights with siblings and classmates. |
| o   low frustration tolerance or infinite patience. | o   low frustration tolerance. |
| o   acting as "mother's little helper." | o   bullying. |

| **Some children experience one extreme . . .** | **. . .while others will experience the exact opposite.** |
|---|---|
| o   impaired concentration spans. | o   excellent academic work. |
| o   difficulty with school work. | o   perfectionist standards (harbouring a tremendous fear of failure). |
| o   poor attendance patterns in school. | o   overly responsible, especially the oldest child. |
| o   clumsy, accident-prone behaviour. | |
| o   fear of attending school. | |
| o   being labelled a "slow learner." | |

## Adolescence (13 + years)

All teenagers are vulnerable to escapist, self-destructive behaviour. Adolescence is a particularly stressful stage and becomes even more acute for those teenagers from a violent home.   The following examples illustrate the most extreme of these behaviours:

o      escape into drug or alcohol abuse.

o      running away from home.

o      escape into pregnancy and early marriage.

o      suicidal thoughts and actions.

o      homicidal thoughts and actions.

o      criminal activities, such as drug-dealing, theft.

Teenagers will continue to differentiate their behaviour along traditional sex lines.

## Young Women

As the daughter of an abusive man enters puberty, he may begin to treat her like a second wife. His jealousies and excessive use of control, usually reserved for his wife, may now be directed towards his daughter. He sometimes is very suspicious of her interest in boys. His suspicious nature may reflect overt incestuous thoughts, if not actual incestuous behaviour.[4] She may hate her own body and feel confused about her sexuality (being female = being like Mom = being punished). She may become sexually promiscuous or withdraw and completely deny her sexuality.

## Young Men

A young man in a violent environment may try to become his mother's protector while his father is in the home. Ironically, if the father leaves the home, this same son often moves into his Dad's footsteps and abuses his mother if he feels she is stepping "out of line." (This most often happens with the oldest child; sometimes if a daughter is the oldest child, she will adopt this role.) The young man may hate his own body and feel confused about his sexuality (being male = being like Dad = being mean and abusive). He may become sexually promiscuous (sons are often encouraged by fathers to "sow their wild oats") or he might withdraw and completely avoid contact with the opposite sex.

## Interviewing the Child

Most children from violent homes do not require long-term counselling. What they do need is information, support and advocacy. A counsellor must be willing to act as the child's advocate. Interviews with children should include exploration of the following areas:

### Presence of Child Abuse

QUESTIONS: **How do people fight in your family? What does your Dad do when he gets mad -- yells, runs away, slams the door, throws things, hits, punches, pushes, kicks? What does your Mom do? What do your sisters and brothers do? What do you do? Do you know what discipline means? When is it used? What kinds of discipline are there in your house? What do you think is a fair punishment if you do something you're not supposed to do? What kinds of things**

---

[4]  Walker, Lenore. The Battered Woman. New York: Harper and Row, 1979.

hurt you (for example, certain words, certain actions, certain thoughts)? What kinds of things make you feel good? Do you know what bad touches are? Good touches? Describe the details and who gives the different touches. Do you ever feel scared of your Mom? Your Dad? Your brothers and sisters? Anyone else in your life? Did you ever try to hurt yourself? Describe the details of what you did.

PURPOSES:
o    to assess the presence of child abuse (sexual, physical, psychological and destruction to property and pets).

o    to assess the presence of self-destructive behaviour.

o    to measure the child's level of fear.

o    to assess the child's safety.

Understanding of Wife Assault

QUESTIONS: Did you ever see your Dad hit your Mom? Describe the details. What did you do? How did you feel? Did you think he was right? Why do you think your Dad is violent? Why do you think your Mom gets hit? Do you think other Dads are violent? Do you think other Moms get hit? Did you ever try to stop your Dad or protect your Mom? How did you do it? Do you think you can stop the violence? Who is responsible for the violence? What do you think your Mom should do? What do you think your Dad should do? What do you think you should do?

PURPOSES:
o    to establish the extent of the child's exposure to the violence.

o    to assess the child's understanding of the violence.

o    to give the counsellor an opportunity to correct and clarify inaccurate information and myths.

Understanding of Separation/Divorce

QUESTIONS: Do you know what a separation is? Have your parents ever separated? How did you feel about it? What is a divorce? Why do people get divorced? Do you think your Mom and Dad will get a divorce? How do you feel about that? What does custody mean? Do you know what access means (if parents are separated and mother has custody)? Do you want to have contact with your Dad? Do you feel safe with your Dad when he visits you? Does your Mom or Dad expect you to pass messages back and forth? How do you feel about that?

PURPOSES:
o    to assess the child's understanding of separation and divorce.

o    to assess the child's ability to deal with his/her reality.

o    to assess the child's reactions to his/her parents' potential or actual separation or divorce.

## Understanding of Protection

QUESTIONS: **Do you know what safety means? Where do you feel safe? When? With whom? Where do you feel unsafe? When? With whom? Do you know what protection means? Do you know what a shelter is? What other safe places do you know about? Do you know what the police officer's job is? Have they ever come to your house? What did they do? Say? Have you ever heard the following words being used: assault charge, peace bond, restraining order, court? What do these words mean? What can your Mom do to protect herself? What can you do to protect yourself? Do you think your Dad will hurt you, your Mom or himself?**

PURPOSES:
o    to help the child understand the importance and meaning of protection and safety.

o    to identify the child's ability to protect him/herself.

o    to help the child understand the legal language she/he might be exposed to.

## Relationship With Parents

QUESTIONS: **What do you like about your Mom? Dad? What do you dislike about your Mom? Dad? Are you close to your Mom? Are you close to your Dad? What kinds of things do you talk about with your Dad? With your Mom? What kinds of things can't you talk about with your Dad? With your Mom? What kinds of things do you do with your Mom? With your Dad? How much time do you spend with your Mom? With your Dad? What do you worry about the most with your Mom? With your Dad? Extend these questions to any important care-giving person in the child's life (for example, aunt, grandfather, foster parent).**

PURPOSES:
o    to assess the kind of relationships the child has with the parents or other care-givers.

o    to assess the degree of attachment with each parent.

## Personal Support System

QUESTIONS: **Who do you talk to when you're upset? Who would you go to if you were in trouble? Tell me about your friends. Do you miss them (if child has** moved)?  What other things have changed in your life?  Can you keep in touch with them?  What kinds of things do you like to do for fun?  Who do you do them with?

PURPOSES:
o      to assess the child's degree of isolation.

o      to assess the level of disruption in the child's life (in the event of separation).

o      to assess the child's access to supportive people.

Child's Feelings

QUESTIONS: What do you like about yourself?  What would you like to change about yourself?  Do you feel sad, depressed, mad, guilty, confused, about what's happening in your family?  What bothers you the most about your situation?  What do you hope the future will bring for you and your family?

PURPOSES:
o      to assess the child's ability to identify and articulate feelings.

o      to identify the child's feelings about him/herself.

o      to identify the child's feelings about him/her situation.

o      to identify the child's hopes for the future.


**The Responsibilities of the Child Advocate Are. . .**

o      to make sure children are not being physically or sexually abused, neglected or deprived of their basic needs.

o      to reassure them it's not their fault.

o      to be willing to take the time to talk with children and give them accurate information about their situation.

o      to create an atmosphere of safety and trust.

o      to dispel destructive myths they have been exposed to.

o      to show children that violence is wrong.

o      to help them learn better ways to deal with their anger (because both of their role models have been ineffective).

o      to help them feel comfortable with themselves.

o      to reassure them it's all right to be angry with their Moms even though the violence is not their Mom's fault.

o      to reassure them it's all right to love their Dads, even though they hate his violent behaviour.

o    to let them know you believe them.

o    to help them sort out their fears, confusion, ambivalence.

o    to help them recognize their rights and their responsibilities.

o    to talk to their teacher or whomever needs to know about their situation.

o    to help them come up with creative solutions to their problems.

o    to help them learn ways to protect themselves.

## Counselling Issues for Children

As outlined earlier, most children do not require long-term intervention. Like their parents, children will benefit most from an opportunity to meet with other children in a group atmosphere. The counselling issues most pressing for children include:

1.    Learning that violence is unacceptable behaviour.

2.    Identification and expression of their feelings, such as anger, guilt, confusion, fear.

3.    Learning constructive ways to deal with their anger and aggression.

4.    Dealing with ambivalence. They may love their Dad but hate his violence. They may love their Mom but feel angry with her for putting up with the violence **or** for leaving.

5.    Role modelling. These children often feel at a loss as to how to act. They can either identify with the aggressor or identify with the victim. Both choices leave them in a difficult position. Alternative role models must be made available to them.

6.    Role reversals. Children (especially the oldest) often try to protect the mother and end up assuming a parenting role in the family.

7.    Internalization of blame. Children often internalize responsibility for the family problems and believe it to be their fault. Like their mother, they mistakenly believe they can control their father's violence by being a better child. They sometimes develop an omnipotent sense of control over the process.

8.    Mourning of losses, such as those brought about by their mother's and father's separation. These include disruption to their routines, changes in schools, losing daily contact with their friends, missing the good parts of their relationship with their father.

9.    Developing more flexible definitions of male and female behaviour than what they were exposed to in their home.

10.   Building a positive self-image.

11.   Learning what their rights and responsibilities are, including such self-

protective actions as calling the police, running to a neighbour's home.

12.    Unmet dependency needs.  These children often have not had time to be children.

### Tips for Child Advocates

1.    Teach mothers to recognize the learning model her children have been exposed to and what she can realistically expect from them.  She must not let their disrespect of her defeat her attempts to change.  It will take time to undo the destructive messages they have learned.  Patience is required and a willingness to continually repeat "violence is no longer acceptable in our home."

2.    If a mother is helped to develop her own positive self-image as well as shown ways to help her child's self-esteem increase, then the child will begin to see a different model.  The effects of the child's past life will lessen.

3.    Assess the reality of a mother's fear that her child may be kidnapped, harmed or used in some destructive way.  The whereabouts of mothers and children **can** sometimes be traced by persistent fathers through ingenious methods such as tracing of school records or manipulating day-care staff.  Reality often dictates that children's lives be disrupted (e.g., change of school, temporary removal from school) in order to enhance the protection of both mothers and their children.  This disruption to a child's life should **always** be documented in detail in the event of a custody or access dispute.

4.    If fathers show any genuine attachment to their children, this should be built on as one way to motivate him to change his behaviour (e.g., "I can see that you really love your children.  Are you aware of how your violent behaviour affects them?").  He may continue to play an active role in their lives even after a separation, so his influence on them must be addressed.  Strategies might include his participation in a fathers' group, learning about the impact of violence on children and establishing clear ground rules during his visits, such as no drinking, no discussion of adult problems, no threats or unrealistic promises.

5.    Do not criticize the father in front of the children.  (This does **not** mean condoning his behaviour.  Violence can be clearly spelled out as wrong and unacceptable.)  Encourage the children to ventilate their anger if they want to, but it is important to withhold any evaluative opinions you may have of him.  Underneath children's anger is usually a layer of confusion and ambivalence.  Often they love their Dad and hope that he loves them.  By putting down their father, you put the child down as well.  The child sees him/herself as part of **both** her/his Mom and Dad.  (For instance, "If Dad is bad then a part of me must be bad too.")  It is also important to assist mothers to understand the negative effects of criticizing the children's father.

6.    Help the child identify at least one significant person in a stable situation, in her/his life that s/he can turn to for support and advice when needed such as a favourite aunt, teacher or neighbour.

7.    A child should **not** be sent off to a play therapist prematurely.  Singling the child out in this way may further the child's mistaken belief that s/he is to blame for all the family problems.  It would be wiser to share your skills with the mother and teach her ways to deal with her child's feelings constructively (such as through puppet play).  This is particularly important for pre-school children.  For older children, an educational support group would be most effective, with a concurrent child-centred group program for mothers.

Children's needs should not be addressed in isolation from those of their families.

8.      When a child's situation has stabilized but excessive symptoms continue (such as self-destructive behaviours - pulling hair out, biting self), this may be the time to consult a child specialist.

9.      Children are resilient. They can cope with yo-yo situations and harsh realities if they are given the facts. What disturbs children the most is not knowing what is going to happen to them, not having their feelings acknowledged and not being treated as important persons. Respect goes a long way in helping them cope with a trying situation.

## What Happens to Children After the Marriage Ends

After a separation occurs, people mistakenly tend to breathe a sigh of relief. Perhaps the offender has finally gotten the message that the marriage has ended. The victim has resolved her ambivalence and is ready to move on in her life. Hopefully, she is no longer in physical danger.

It is crucial that the abuse not be continued through the children. They are not pawns and should not become the parents' weapons to continue hurting each other. Fathers, most likely as a way of continuing to abuse the mother, threaten to kidnap the children, make terrorizing calls and harass mothers about visits, access or support and pursue long, torturous custody battles. This is all emotionally exhausting and no one wins. Usually mothers get custody.

The father should be assessed to see if his desire for contact with the children is legitimate. The quality of his parenting bond should have been assessed by now. If there is any genuine interest in the children, it is in their best interest to have this fostered. They are a part of him. Children usually want to have some form of contact with their Dad, once their fear is alleviated. The better able he is to relate to the children, the better for them. If there is concern for either the mother's safety or the child's safety, visits or exchanges must be supervised by a reliable third party.

Mediation can only be effective if the violence has ended and the intimidation has stopped. This usually can only stop if he has gone through a group program and realizes his responsibility for his behaviour. It is a waste of time to expect cooperation between a couple on parenting issues or property settlements if the husband is still able to induce fear and use intimidation tactics to get his way. The power imbalance is too great to pursue joint work. The same rules that have been previously applied to marriage counselling are applicable here as well.

Mediators must be trained to recognize the effects of violence on mothers and children. Where wife assault has still not been addressed and resolved (with the victim safe, the children safe and the offender changed) mediation is too dangerous!

**Violent men cannot be good fathers until their abusive, intimidating behaviour ceases!**

**Suggested Reading -- Working with Children**

. . . . and then we went to a safe place. A Training Manual for Children's Services in Battered Women's Shelters. Available from: Project for Victims of Family Violence, P.O. Box 2915, Fayetteville, Arkansas 72702. Cost $15.00 (U.S.) includes postage.

Briggs, Dorothy. Your Child's Self-Esteem. New York: Doubleday, 1970.

Canfield, Jack, and Wells, H. 100 Ways to Enhance Self-Concept in the Classroom. New Jersey: Prentice-Hall, 1976.

Gordon Janine Drucker. What To Do with the Children. Available from: Council on Battered Women, P.O. Box 54737, Atlanta, Georgia, 30308. Cost $17.50 (U.S.) includes postage.

Judson, Stephanie. A Manual on Non-Violence and Children. Available from: Non-violence and Children, 1515 Cherry Street, Philadelphia, Pennsylvania, 19102.

Miller, Maureen. To Share with Your Children. Niles, Illinois: Argus Communication DLM Inc., 1978.

Miller, Maureen. Family Communication: Keeping Connected in a Time of Change. Niles, Illinois: Argus Communication DLM Inc., 1978. Both of these books should be at your public library.

Pogrebin, Letty. Growing Up Free -- Raising Your Child in the 80's. New York: Bantam Books, 1980.

Sopp-Gilson, Susan. "Children From Violent Homes." Journal of Ontario Association of Children's Aid Societies 3:10, (December, 1980), pp. 1-10.

They're So Cute When They're Little. Shelter Children's Program Manual by Michele Aiken, Central California Alliance Against Domestic Violence. Available from: Western Centre on Domestic Violence, 870 Market Street, Suite 1058, San Francisco, C.A. 94102. Cost $6.50 (U.S.) includes postage.

Westra, Bonnie, and Martin, Harold. "Children of Battered Women." Maternal-

Child Nursing Journal 10:1 (Spring, 1981), pp. 41-54.

Wolfe, David, et al. "The Impact of Violence Upon Children's Adjustment." London, Ontario:  University of Western Ontario, 1984.

Wolfe, David, et al. "Children of Battered Women:  The Relation Between Child Behavior, Family Violence and Maternal Stress." London, Ontario: University of Western Ontario, 1984.

**Suggested Resources -- Working with Children**

Anagnost, Eloise, et al. Children in Shelters:  A Resource Guide for Family Violence Programs. Available from:  Domestic Violence Project, P.O. Box 7052, Ann Arbour, Michigan 48107.  Cost $2.00 (U.S.) includes postage.

Family Face Puppets - used in role-playing. (Instruction #1185).  Available from:  Moyer/The Teachers' Store, Moyer/The Teachers' Store, 25 Milvan Drive, Weston, Ontario M9L 1Z1. (from their catalogue).

Farah, Bobbie. The Angry Book - Colouring Book. Available from:  Domestic Violence Project, P.O. Box 7052, Ann Arbour, Michigan 48107.  Cost $1.50 (U.S.) includes postage.

Gardner, Richard M.D. Books and diagnostic/therapeutic instruments available from:  Creative Therapeutics, P.O. Box R, Cresskill, New Jersey 07626.

Hilt, Joy. Ready Set Grow. Educational Products Vivision Word Inc., Waco, Texas 76703.  Available from:  Louise Kool and Son, 1147 Bellamy Road, Unit 6, Scarborough, Ontario M1H 1H6.  Tel:  1-800-268-4011.

Understanding Our Feelings.   Set of 28 black-and-white photos to explore emotions.  Available from:  Moyer/The Teachers' Store, 25 Milvan Drive, Weston, Ontario M9L 1Z1. (from their catalogue).

**Books for Children***

Annie, Once I Was A Little Bit Frightened. Book on sexual abuse available from:  The Rape and Abuse Crisis Center, P.O. Box 1655, Fargo, North Dakota 58107.

---

\*      I am grateful to the efforts of Gail Clarke, child care worker from Niagara's Women In Crisis Shelter, who drew together many of these books and resources.

Blume, Judy. It's Not the End of the World. Scarsdale, N.Y.: Bradbury Press, 1972.

Davis, Dianne. Something Is Wrong at My House. Parenting Press, 7750 31st Ave. N.E. Seattle, Washington 98115.

Despert, J. Louise. Children of Divorce. New York: Doubleday, 1962.

Gardner, Richard A. The Boy's and Girl's Book about Divorce. New York: Bantam, 1970.

Grollman, Earl A. (ed.). Explaining Divorce to Children. Boston: Beacon Press, 1969.

Gustav, Susan. When I Visit Daddy or Daddy Visits Me. Before We Are Six, 12 Bridgeport Rd. E., Waterloo, Ontario.

He Told Me Not To Tell. Book on sexual abuse available from: King County Rape Relief, 305 So. 43rd., Renton, W.A. 98055.

Kalt, Jonah, and David Viscott, M.D. What Every Kid Should Know. Haughton Mifflin, 1974.

LeShan, Eda. What Makes Me Feel This Way? Collier Books, 1972.

Richards, Arlene, and Irene Willis. How To Get It Together When You Are Coming Apart. New York: David McKay & Co., 1976.

Red Flag, Green Flag People. Colouring book sexual abuse available from: Rape and Abuse Crisis Center, P.O. Box 1655, Fargo, North Dakota 58107.

Robson, Bonnie, M.D. My Parents Are Divorced Too. Toronto: Dorset, 1979.

Simon, Norma. All Kinds of Families. Chicago: Albert Whitman & Company, 1976.

Sinberg, Janet. Divorce is a Grown Up Problem. Avon Books, 1978.

Smith, Doris Buchanan. Kick a Stone Home. New York: Thomas Y. Crowell, 1974.

## Books for Parents

Gardner, Richard A. The Parent's Book About Divorce. New York: Bantam, 1977.

## 7 SUPPORT GROUPS FOR ASSAULTED WOMEN

by Susan Harris

Short-term counselling is sufficient for **most** assaulted women to make the desired and necessary changes in their lives. **A combination of individual and group sessions is the best way to facilitate her <u>change</u>.**

This chapter addresses several commonly asked questions about groups for assaulted women. A group format that I have successfully used is presented, along with a description of the group process that occurs.

Various types of group formats have been used by others working in this area. The qualitative difference between these groups and traditional therapy groups is in **the emphasis on peer support.** Assaulted wives are **not** perceived as in need of long-term therapy. They are perceived as needing access to the information, protection and support necessary to achieve an end to the abuse in their lives.

### Why a Group is Important

1.	Becoming a member of a group for assaulted women enables a woman to name her abusive experience. **The identification of herself as an assaulted woman is the first step** she takes in no longer covering up or denying the pain of being a victim. This identification begins the process of overcoming her victimization.

2.	**The group is a safe place** where members are encouraged to tell their stories of assault and oppression. They are able to identify that they have been victims without the imposition of shame or guilt. They are believed.

3.	Isolation is broken down as individual women realize that **they are not the only ones.** The benefits of this sharing of common experience can not be overemphasized. As women listen to each others' stories they will inevitably say, "I thought that kind of thing only happened to me." Tremendous relief comes with knowledge that the seemingly bizarre events in your life are not yours alone. You are not crazy, bad or to be blamed for being assaulted.

4.	**The group provides positive support.** Most assaulted women have experienced unhelpful responses from friends, family or professionals. As women in the group confront their own attitudes about wife abuse, they are able to support each other's efforts to end the violence in their lives. The group decreases dependence on professional help as the women develop their own mutual aid system.

5.	**The group is energizing.** As women being to work together to change their lives, their collective efforts produce an energizing force that surpasses what can happen in individual sessions.

6.	**The group becomes a viable source of protection** for its members, by providing realistic feedback, sharing resources and broadening personal support networks.

## Why is a Leader Important?

1.   In a group of assaulted women, **the potential for crisis is high.** It is important for the group to have someone who can calmly assess the danger in every situation, provide the best information on available resources and assist in working out safe alternatives.

2.   A leader also acts as a role model, challenging societal attitudes about wife assault with her own beliefs.

3.   The leader provides consistency in the group's values. The leader's consistent stance that women have a right to live free from assault and that they have the ability to change their situations facilitates group movement from identification to action.

## What Does a Leader Need to Know Before Starting a Support Group?

A group leader needs to **understand the social context** in which wife assault occurs. She needs to be aware of the effects of traditional sex role socialization and the impact of living in a male-dominated society. This social analysis allows the leader to address the myths that surround wife assault, express helpful values and assist the group understanding that individual abusive experiences are part of women's second-class status.

The leader must also believe that **women working together actively can give each other the support and encouragement needed to overcome their victimization.** This is sometimes called empowerment. This belief in the ability of assaulted women to help each other creates a positive force in the atmosphere of the group. Excitement comes from the group conviction that assaulted women **can** develop the confidence necessary to stop being victims of abuse!

A leader also needs to understand the process of victimization that occurs for a woman in an abusive relationship. In this regard, personal experience of assault is an asset. If the leader has successfully worked through her own experience of assault, personal disclosure provides powerful role modelling.

However, the majority of women have experienced some form of victimization. The important ingredient is the empathic connection to these experiences. To achieve this connection, try the following exercise.

## Victimization Exercise*

Remember an incident in which you were a victim, a situation in which you were not in control. What is happening is what you do not want to happen.

---

*   Conroy, Kathryn. "Victimization Exercise." Presented during a workshop on Treatment Issues with Battered Women. Toronto, May 7-8, 1981.

(Examples: rape, robbery, assault, humiliation at work, harassment on the street.)

Consider the following questions as they relate to your experience of victimization.

1. What happened?

2. What did you think about while it happened?

3. Who did you tell?

4. Who did you not tell?

5. How did you feel?

6. What did you do?

7. What effects lingered?

8. What were the long-term effects?

9. What is it like to remember it now?

The goal of this exercise is to assist the recognition of our own potential to be victims and to decrease the distance we put between ourselves and assaulted women.

In your answers, look for the commonalities between your response and that of an abused wife. Did you respond to your experience of victimization with "Why me?" thoughts, helpless feelings, or self blame for allowing the incident to happen? Were there any surprises in who you told and who you did not tell? (Many people may not tell their families because, despite prevailing myths to the contrary, they may not find their families supportive.) Any surprises in what you did? What were the effects? Examine conflicting feelings, such as anger versus guilt. It is a common reaction to want to feel in control. This quasi-control is maintained by feeling responsible even though you had no **real** control over the event.

Were you fearful? Now multiply this experience by the number of days an abused wife has been in her situation of victimization.

By connecting to her own experiences of victimization, the leader will have empathy for assaulted women. This empathy permits the leader to respond with respect and caring to the group members while they learn to act in self-protecting ways. It also teaches the leader the patience required to allow an assaulted woman to move at her own pace.

To be an effective resource, a leader must also have a practical knowledge of an assaulted wife's legal options. A thorough knowledge of available local services is mandatory. It is advisable to have already established a network of sympathetic referral sources for legal, medical, financial, housing and child welfare needs.

A leader will require advocacy skills to assist group members in negotiating with unresponsive institutions. The amount of advocacy required will depend on the attitudes of the local community's services. Before establishing a group, awareness of local attitudes helps the leader give the group members realistic information on what they may expect and how best to deal with unhelpful service responses.

### Can Men Lead Groups for Assaulted Women?

**No.** Only women can lead groups for assaulted women. Although men may understand the social context of wife assault and demonstrate great sensitivity to victims of violence, male group leaders are counterproductive for two main reasons:

1.    An assaulted wife goes through a process of being fearful and then angry at men. The closest man in her life has victimized her. She needs to be able to get angry about it! A male group leader inhibits this process.

2.    Wife abuse happens to women. An assaulted wife needs to learn to trust that **she** can protect herself. This best happens through the modelling of a female leader, who with confidence and assertiveness shows that women can act to take care of themselves.

### What are the Advantages of Co-Leading?

Ideally, a support group for assaulted women should be co-led for the following reasons:

1.    Co-leading decreases the stress on an individual leader. Crisis can be more effectively managed if there are two sources of consistent support.

2.    Debriefing between leaders after each session allows the opportunity to review if all alternatives have been explored in situations related to individual members' safety. Also a review of the group process helps planning to keep the group's movement on track.

3.    Co-leading diffuses the power inherent in a leadership position. Effective sharing of leadership illustrates women's capacity to share responsibility while working toward a common goal.

One potential resource for a co-leader is an assaulted woman who has completed a previous group. This would be a woman who demonstrates natural helping skills and who has successfully worked through her own experience of victimization. Her presence in the group provides strong encouragement for the other women that change is indeed achievable.

## What are the Group Goals?

The group goals follow from a well-defined philosophical position. The message, made clear initially by the leaders, is abuse is not to be tolerated. The primary purpose of the group is to support the women in taking the necessary steps to ensure they will no longer be victims of abuse. Group goals are:

o    women can take responsibility for protecting themselves.

o    women can take responsibility for improving their own lives.

Leaving or not leaving the violent relationship is **not** the issue. If a woman chooses to remain in her situation, this choice must be respected. The important decision is the decision to act self-protectively. To act self-protectively is to decide not to be abused any more.

## A Group Format

The group format may be best described as a combination of problem-solving and education. The group is time-limited. The ten weekly sessions are closed to new membership after the third session. Experience with open groups suggests that the continuous intake of new members makes it difficult to move beyond the identification stage.

The group begins with a brief check-in period. Each member is asked to report on their safety, the action they have taken to meet the group goals and any issues that are emerging. During check-ins, individual problem-solving time is requested by the members (or may be suggested by the leaders if viewed as necessary to a member's safety). Priority within the group is given to any woman in crisis.

Safety concerns are handled by developing a plan of action that offers the woman the most protection. All members are encouraged to develop protection plans along with setting their own goals to improve their life situations.

The meeting time (roughly two to three hours, depending on the size of the group) is divided into individual problem-solving time and discussion of topics selected by the group members. How this time is divided should be flexible and adapted to the group members' need for problem discussion. In practice there tends to be a great deal of overlap between topics discussed and individual issues.

At the end of each session the leaders should make sure that closure has occurred. Some type of checking out procedure can be initiated. No woman should leave the group with an unresolved crisis. If a member has an intense emotional reaction to a topic presented, spend extra time with her at the end of the session to achieve some resolution.

### What are Some Important Topics to Cover?

Topics most regularly chosen by groups I have worked with are:

1. <u>Fear</u>

Most assaulted women cope with their abusive partners by denying or minimizing the amount of fear they experience. Once in the group, openly identified as assaulted wives, these fears emerge and need to be discussed realistically. Some husbands harass their wives unmercifully after a separation. Others make many threats that they do not carry out. Danger is not minimized but emphasis is placed on not becoming immobilized by fear.

An important way of alleviating fear is to provide accurate resource information and realistic feedback. One method to get at fears is to have each group member develop a "Worst Fears List."*

---

### SAMPLE - WORST FEARS LIST

**WORST FEAR:** Bob will kidnap the children.

| <u>Reasons it is likely</u> | <u>Reasons it is unlikely</u> |
|---|---|
| He's threatened to do it. | I have custody. |
| He wants to get back at me. | He never wanted to babysit, so I don't think he'll want full-time responsibility. |
| He says he loves the children and wants them with him. | I've spoken with the children about what to do. |
| | The school has been informed about their situation. |
| | I don't leave them unattended. |

---

* Ginny, NiCarthy. <u>Getting Free</u>. Seattle, Washington: Seal Press, 1982, pp. 56-57.

The group can then help in reviewing the lists.  Are the likely and unlikely reasons realistic?  Have all available resources been considered?

When fears are identified, the next step is the development of protective plans of action to deal concretely with particular fears.  A protection plan may look like this:

---

### SAMPLE – PROTECTION PLAN

FEAR:      Bob wants to meet me to discuss access to the children. I'm afraid he will threaten me (or be violent).  I'm afraid I will be intimidated and not stand up for what I want.

PLAN:      I will rehearse what to say to him beforehand.  I will stick to the topic of access and refuse to discuss anything else.  I will arrange to meet him in a public place.  I will have Mary drive me there and sit close by.  She will have the number of the police to call if Bob threatens or strikes me.  I will leave with Mary and she will spend the night at my house.

| Disadvantages | Advantages |
| --- | --- |
| I may be persuaded to change my mind. | I will feel safer having others around. |
| I may be embarrassed if Bob causes a scene. | Mary will call the police if necessary. |
| | I will be able to say what I want, face to face. |

---

The advantages and disadvantages of protection plans should be carefully reviewed by the group.  Have all the options been considered?  In the proceeding example an alternate plan could be **not** to meet with her husband at all and tell him to direct any questions about access to her lawyer.

Remember assaulted women are the experts on what works and what does not.  They will be able to see the flaws in each others' plans. The leaders' job is to make sure all the key issues are covered.  For instance, in the above example it would be important for the leader to have a comprehensive picture of Bob's history of violence in order to address her safety issues.  If the leader believed she was endangering herself, the leader must realistically share her opinion with the group and suggest alternatives, although the final choice always rests with the woman.

Group members can also actively assist each other with fear by sharing phone numbers and spending time together when one's fears are especially intense.

2.  Anger

Anger is a healthy, normal reaction for someone who has been victimized. However, assaulted women have not been allowed to express this anger. Most have internalized the anger they feel into "depressed" or "self-blaming" feelings. Some have developed self-destructive ways, such as the abuse of alcohol and/or drugs to drown their anger. Others may have attempted suicide or developed psychiatric symptoms.

Traditional female role conditioning teaches women that "nice ladies don't get angry." This has often been brutally reinforced by a spouse who reacts to any sign of self-assertion with violence. To identify ways the group members have masked their anger and to develop safe alternatives, the following exercise may be used.

---

**SAMPLE - ANGER EXERCISE**
**Ways I Have Covered Up My Anger**

| | |
|---|---|
| Feeling depressed | Yelling at the children |
| Withdrawing | Drinking too much |

**Safe Ways to Express the Anger I Feel**

| | |
|---|---|
| Talking about it in the group | Practising being assertive |
| Asking for what I want | Saying "No" |

---

It is crucial that assaulted women identify the ways they have masked their anger and begin to view anger as an acceptable emotion. It is her anger that will motivate her self-protection. It is her anger that says, "I won't let you do that to me again!"

**It is her anger that will save her life.**

Anger is presented as an energizing force that can be tapped to lead to action. Healthy anger is distinguished from revenge, rage and aggression. The leaders' role in making this distinction is discussed later in the description of the group process.

In order to get angry, assaulted women need to believe they have rights.

The following "Bill of Rights" may be used to start the group re-thinking their own attitudes toward themselves.

Increased assertiveness on the part of an assaulted wife may increase the hostility of the violent spouses. For women who are still with their spouses, the leaders should explore the realistic consequences of this with her. This does **not** mean than an assaulted wife should be silenced. It does mean that the consequences of assertive communication should be prepared for. She should have a plan of action to deal with any anticipated abuse.

---

### BILL OF RIGHTS FOR ASSAULTED WOMEN*

o     I have the right not to be abused.

o     I have the right to anger over past beatings.

o     I have the right to change the situation.

o     I have the right to freedom from fear of abuse.

o     I have the right to request and expect assistance from police or social agencies.

o     I have the right to share my feelings and not be isolated from others.

o     I have the right to want a better role model of communication for my children.

o     I have the right to be treated like an adult.

o     I have the right to leave the abusive environment.

o     I have the right to privacy.

o     I have the right to express my own thoughts and feelings.

o     I have the right to develop my individual talents and abilities.

o     I have the right to legally prosecute the abusing spouse.

o     I have the right not to be perfect.

---

*     Patricia G. Ball and Elizabeth Wyman, "Battered Wives and Powerlessness: What Can Counsellors Do?" Victimology: An International Journal, Vol. 2, 1977-78, February, 1978.

### 3. Sexuality

For most assaulted wives, some form of sexual abuse has been part of the assaultive experience. This can range from rape to put downs about her sexual ability. Since many women do not discuss this aspect of wife abuse readily, it is helpful to have sexuality as a topic.

Information on female sexuality, such as the book Woman's Experience of Sex, by Sheila Kitzinger, helps women redefine their notions about themselves as sexual beings and provides a beginning toward developing a more positive body image.

### 4. Legal Issues

All assaulted women should have accurate information on their legal rights, whether they are choosing to take legal action or not. Many group members will probably be already involved in the legal system. For this topic, if at all possible, bring in a sympathetic female lawyer who has experience in this area.

Other topics frequently chosen for which an outside resource person may be appropriate include:

### 5. Police

What assaulted women can expect from police and how can they better help them. Resource: an empathetic female officer.

### 6. Characteristics of the Abuser

Resource: a leader of a group for men who batter.

### 7. The Impact of Violence on Children

Resource: a child care worker from a shelter.

### 8. Alcohol and Violence

Resource: a sympathetic chemical dependency worker.

Keep in mind: **NEVER USE A RESOURCE PERSON WHO DOES NOT ACCEPT THE GROUP PHILOSOPHY.** Also, **do not overuse** resource people. Two or three per group is sufficient. Too many outside resources may inhibit the group's development of cohesiveness. The women are there to work together to solve problems, not to attend a lecture series. Instead, it is better for the leaders to research the topic and present it themselves. Films may be used as effective tools for discussion. Films are available from the Family Violence Prevention Program (see Appendix F).

9.    Starting Your Own Life

Some variation of this theme is possible towards the end of the group.  This topic is really an evaluation of:

o    where the women have been.

o    where they are now.

o    where they want to be in the future.

The women have the opportunity to review the dramatic changes they have made.  Some observations that I, as a leader, have made about women's changes during the course of a group are illustrated in the following examples:

1.    When Jennifer came to see me she was already separated but so fearful, she was unable to look me in the eye.  She had been so intimidated she lowered her eyelids rather than risk eye contact.  By the time Jennifer completed the group she had become a fiery spokesperson for assaulted women.  She attended public meetings and was able to speak out freely about what she and other women needed.

2.    After several contacts with my agency's after-hours emergency phone service, Margaret was persuaded to come in for an appointment.  She wanted to separate from her violent husband but was terrified.  The group gave her the courage to leave her situation.  She relocated to another city and is now working with their local shelter.

3.    Diane coped with living with a violent, alcoholic spouse by drinking with him.  By the time she got to the group she had developed a drinking problem of her own.  Diane was able to use the group to support her in separating.  After ending the abuse in her life Diane was able to confront her drinking and joined Alcoholics Anonymous.

4.    Mary entered the group with the desire to remain in her marriage.  She had given up her career to stay at home to try and please her husband.  The group helped Mary maintain the courage to insist that her husband enter a group for men who abuse their wives.  He did and Mary went back to work, this time to please herself.

Groups for Native, Francophone and Immigrant assaulted women should include topics that are **culturally relevant** to their situations.  Leaders should be from the particular groups in question and demonstrate strong cultural identities and thorough awareness of the special concerns of these women.

---

### SAMPLE - GROUP GROUND RULES

A contract of ground rules can help the leaders in defining a group structure. These are presented by the leaders at the first meeting for group agreement. A typical contract I have used follows:

1. This group will meet regularly once a week for ten weeks.

2. Each session begins promptly at an agreed-upon time.

3. **The group closes at the third session;** no one may join at that time who has not attended a previous session.

4. **The group is committed at the third session;** each person pledges at this session to continue the entire course of the group without absence except for extreme emergency.

5. **Confidentiality is required.** Everything discussed in groups must be held in confidence, both within and outside the group, forever. Members are not to discuss personal information shared in the sessions with anyone.

6. **There is respect for each other's choices.** Members do not rescue each other (that is, force a member to do anything she is not ready to do or try to make her decisions for her).

7. Members give each other their total attention when one is speaking.

8. **Priority within the group is given to any member in crisis.**

---

### A Description of the Group Process

Overcoming the victimization of wife assault is a process. One theory that helps explain how assaulted women change as individuals and as a group is the "Dependency Cycle" (See Figure 1).

The stages in the dependency cycle reflect life positions assumed in response to one's social condition, i.e., the opportunities, rights and availability of choices one experiences in society. As one moves out of dependency, there are definable stages one must pass through before achieving interdependence. This is a cycle of growth.

## DEPENDENCY CYCLE*

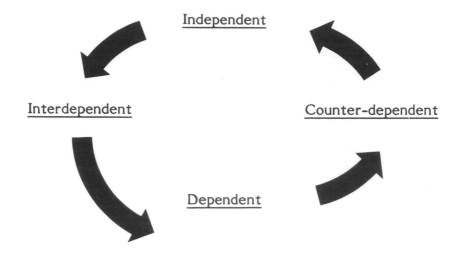

Independent

Interdependent          Counter-dependent

Dependent

Dependence is a victim position.  The oppression the assaulted woman has experienced is internalized.  She does not feel good about herself and believes the abuse is either deserved, her fault or a fact of life she must accept.  She denies and minimizes the abuse to cope with her fear.

Counter-dependence is a stage of rebellion.  She realizes that she has been oppressed.  The assaulted woman still does not feel good about herself, but she now firmly believes she does **not** deserve abuse.  She is angry!  Angry at the man who has abused her and angry at society for allowing this to happen to her.

Independence is a stage where the assaulted woman is most concerned about her own needs.  She has successfully stood up for herself and her self-image is improved.  She now sees she has choices and opportunities.  She feels good about herself and is protective of her hard-won independence.  If she is in a relationship, she is less concerned about working on it and more concerned about her individual goals.  If she is out of her relationship, she is cautious about new commitments.

Interdependence is a position where trusting relationships are possible. The assaulted woman is now comfortable with her ability to be independent. Her self-esteem is on solid ground.  She is able to consider relationships without

---

*    Nola Symor, "The Dependency Cycle:  Implications for Theory, Therapy and Social Action," <u>Transactional Analysis Journal</u> 7:1 (January, 1977).

fear, knowing that she will act to take care of herself is she is ever abused again.

The passage through these stages is different for every woman. It is possible to get stuck at one stage for a time or move forward then backward between two stages. After this cycle is worked through on wife assault, it may need to be worked through on other issues (such as childhood sexual abuse). Each woman's timing is different and must be respected.

Most assaulted women begin the groups in the dependent life position or fluctuating between dependence and counter-dependence. Some will start in the group in the counter-dependent position.

The aim of the group process is to move the women at least one stage further. It is not intended that women remain at the counter-dependent stage but it is necessary for them to get to that position in order to embrace the two group goals. **Assaulted women must get angry** to choose to no longer be victims of abuse.

Some women, of course, will be able to get to the third position in the cycle, independence, while in the support group. Others will require individual counselling, other kinds of group or life experiences to get to this position and then eventually to interdependence.

To illustrate the group process and the role of the leaders in facilitating it, the life of the group is divided into phases, beginning, middle and ending:

Beginning (Sessions 1-4)

In the beginning phase, the majority of group members will be struggling with the dependent position. They are giving up the denial and minimization they have used to cope with the violence in their lives. Fear and the pain associated with their victimization are the dominant emerging emotions.

Due to the danger of immobilization and the real safety concerns, the leaders initially play a highly visible role. The leaders provide structure and demonstrate confidence and assertiveness. They believe the women's stories, attend to crisis, suggest possible protective action and show faith in the women's ability to change their lives.

The leaders are also clear about their own attitudes. They supportively confront statements that reflect the group members' internalized blame for the violence. They assist the women in coming to terms with the fact that they have no control over the abuser's behaviour by encouraging them to plan for and take responsibility for their own safety.

During the beginning phase, the isolation that is so much a part of wife assault situations is breaking down through the contact with other women in the group. The leaders need to facilitate these connections between members by modelling the giving of affection and encouraging group members to reach out to each other.

A simple caring touch on the arm or a reassuring phrase from the leaders signals to the other women in the group that it is safe to express emotions here. We can be gentle with each other's pain while encouraging action to overcome it.

Leaders can be comfortable with showing their genuine feelings and reactions. It is appropriate to express sadness or anger in response to a woman's story of pain, as long as the leaders remain in control. The message is consistent: with support every woman can change her situation.

In order to move on to the counter-dependent position the group needs to **transform fear into anger.** This is the key to the group's success.

To assist this process the leaders encourage every sign of rebellion. Rebellion may take several forms. It is important that the leaders acknowledge what is courageous for every woman in the group. Some examples are:

o    a woman is able to say "I don't deserve his abuse."

o    a woman has an educational session with a lawyer to find out her legal rights.

o    a woman tells her friends and family what's really been going on.

o    a woman presses assault charges.

o    a woman arranges day-care so she can attend an up-grading course.

o    a woman refuses to stop attending the group even though her husband demands it.

Every assertive act builds the group's confidence. The leaders encourage the acceptance and expression of anger. They may themselves show anger in the group if they hear about abuse. "You don't deserve that. It makes me angry to hear that he did that to you!"

Leaders should make sure that anger does not get misdirected at the victim. It is destructive to blame her and if this occurs in the group it must be addressed.

The leaders need to anticipate much ambivalence as the group moves from dependence to counter-dependence. A member's ambivalence should be identified and dealt with in a non-judgmental way. Ambivalence about making a decision about a relationship is normal. Assaulted women are no exception.

The leaders' role is to assist a woman in weighing the pros and cons of a decision. What are the woman's own needs? What are the benefits she derives from the relationship? She may have financial security, shared child care, a reliable sex partner who is sometimes a good companion. She may like her spouse's family or not want to uproot the children from their neighbourhood. The reasons for staying in any relationship may be numerous. These benefits must be weighed against the costs. The cost is her physical and emotional well-being, and that of her children. The cost may be her ability to choose the direction of her life: to go to school, to get a job. Ultimately the cost could be her life itself.

Each woman's situation is different. The pros and cons of choices need to be clarified within the group but the woman's decision is always respected.

If the leaders feel a woman is making an unsafe decision, this should be pointed out. You cannot force a woman to act but you can clearly state your concern for her. Help her set limits for change to occur. If a husband is promising to do something about his behaviour, suggest a time frame. For example: Bob will contact a counsellor within one week. He will stay in counselling for three months or I will press assault charges.

## Middle (Sessions 5-8)

In the middle phase, the group is at the counter-dependent position. The major emotion expressed is anger. The leaders need to withdraw the control they provided at the beginning of the group. They take on the task of encouraging emotional monitoring so that anger becomes an energizing force. Rage, revenge and aggression are identified as traps.

Monitoring the anger in the group includes normalizing the violent thoughts and feelings the women may be experiencing. It is normal to think you would like to kill the man who has abused you. It is normal to feel vengeful and enraged. However, thinking and feeling such intense anger does **not** mean acting on it.

The leaders act to contain unhelpful expressions of anger within the group. Such expressions may be ventilated while the leaders calmly respond, "It is all right to feel that way given what has happened to you. Now, how can you make that anger work for you? What can you do for yourself that is safe and that you will feel good about?"

Leaders should pay special attention to any situations where they are concerned a woman may act on her aggressive thoughts. A minority of assaulted women do end up killing their spouses in self-defense. If you are concerned that this is a possibility with one of your group members, do not be afraid to raise it. Help her face the consequences of such an act and see that there are alternatives.

Consciousness raising at this stage is an effective way to redirect anger. Women can safely be angry at the social institutions that perpetuate wife abuse. The development of a perspective that gives women a right to equal status in relationships also encourages the group to take responsibility for their rights, collectively and as individuals.

With anger focussed for positive energy, the group experiences increased success in taking responsibility for improving their lives. With each other's support the women are learning they can carry out protective action. They can choose not to be victims of abuse.

Women will lay assault charges or initiate legal actions. Women who were in abusive relationships at the beginning of the group will decide to leave or demand that their spouses enter counselling. The group members are acting as role models for each other. Every success is inspiration for the entire group.

A member's return to an abusive relationship at this phase may be disheartening for herself and the group. In order not to lose this member, it is important to point out what she has achieved. Even attending the group represents a great act of courage. If respect for individual choice and timing has been emphasized throughout the sessions, the group will be able to accept this woman's decision without losing the group's momentum.

If the woman's relationship ends, its loss must be mourned for her to move to the independent stage. No abusive relationship was all bad; there were some good times. Anger is replaced with sadness while hope for an idealized relationship is given up. Leaders can facilitate the mourning process by identifying what is happening and encouraging the examination of the loss.

Independence is also reached through the continued enhancement of self-esteem. The members are encouraged to set attainable goals for themselves. Goals might include:

o    getting a driver's license.

o    establishing credit or a separate bank account.

o    pursuing a talent, such as painting or writing.

o    finishing high school.

o    becoming physically fit.

The goals may be large or small. The importance is that they reflect the woman's desires for herself. The group provides the place where aspirations may be explored without criticism. She is encouraged to examine her potential and make plans to realize her dreams.

Ending (Sessions 9 and 10)

The time-limited nature of the group necessitates discussion of termination as a matter of course during sessions. Members should be reminded every week what session it is and how many sessions are left. Facilitating planning for what will happen for individual members once the group ends is an ongoing function of leadership. For example, after a successful individual problem-solving experience within the group, a woman may be asked, "How will you handle that situation once the group is finished?"

The leaders' presence in the group is increased during the ending phase. Since individual members will be at different stages in the dependency cycle, working out options for when the group ends and dealing with feelings associated with the group's termination are tasks that the leaders must ensure are completed.

Options for "where to go from here" should be relevant to the individual women's goals. Some possible options are:

1.    Personal growth -- individual or group therapy, self-help groups, couple counselling or couples group (for women who decide to remain with their spouses), additional support group work on other issues (such as childhood sexual abuse), physical development (such as self-defense training), and life-style adjustments.

2.    Political activity -- involvement in public speaking and social action efforts on the issue of wife assault.

3.    Career Development -- vocational training, education, volunteer work, re-entering paid work force, career change.

The previous discussion offers illustration of how a group may be structured and how the group process can proceed. Once the decision has been made to form a group, the next step is finding and screening membership.

**How Are Group Referrals Developed**

General advertising in the community is not a particularly effective way to find members. Many abused women do not identify themselves as such. Others are embarrassed and ashamed to talk about the violence in their relationships. Referrals are more likely to come from word of mouth through aware and concerned service providers and community members. This means that your group will have to be credible to those people.

Building referral networks translates into selling the value of support groups for assaulted women. Groups have to be promoted because most women do not initially view them as helpful. To recruit referral sources for your group, you may consider training sessions, public education talks and one-to-one consultations. Certainly the best referral source in your community, if it exists, will be the emergency shelter and/or crisis line for abused women.

If you already work in a service agency, most referrals may initially come from your own caseload. By developing systems of case identification with your colleagues you will also assist their referrals to your group.

## Who Can Benefit from a Support Group?

Most assaulted wives **can** benefit from a support group. This includes women who may require ongoing support once the group is finished. Your assessment will determine if a group is the best source of intervention at this time.

Woman who have a long-term history of abuse, including childhood sexual abuse, can benefit. Women who have developed chemical dependencies as a way of coping with their situations can benefit. Women with psychiatric histories can also benefit. In fact, it may be necessary for these women to deal with the wife assault issue first, before they have the belief in themselves and the energy to deal with these other issues.

Woman who are still in or wanting to return to assaultive relationships can benefit from the group experience. If the group's goals are defined in the way earlier described, being in or wanting out of the relationship are **not** the criteria for admission. A woman can choose to take protective action and thereby not tolerate abuse while in her relationship. The group supports her choice not to be abused without deciding on the future of her relationship. That choice is hers.

Women who have separated or wish to separate from assaultive relationships benefit from the ongoing encouragement necessary to maintain this decision.

## How Are Members Screened?

Screening for group membership should be viewed as an engagement process. It may take several individual interviews to help a woman identify her victimization and perceive a group as a way to support change in her life. The provision of crisis intervention and resource information during this period will give a woman reason to have confidence that the leaders can provide a safe atmosphere.

Some techniques for engaging an assaulted woman are:

o    encourage her to come to just one or two sessions and give her the power of deciding if the group can be helpful.

o    help women who are still in abusive relationships to work out a safe way to attend the group.

o    assure her that if she decides not to talk, her decision will be respected.

o    offer assistance with child care and transportation.

o    ensure confidentiality.

o    emphasize educational aspect, such as knowing your rights and available resources.

Developing a group membership that is most effective depends on having a mix of women at various stages.  If it is possible to have two or three members who are already at the anger stage, they will greatly assist the group's movement to this position.  Consider also how the women may serve as role models to each other.  A woman who has already left a violent partner provides immediate motivation to one who is wanting to leave.

Only those women who would feel extremely threatened by a group or those that the leaders assess to be potentially highly disruptive need to be screened out.  Not very many women will fall into these categories.  For those that do, make sure you have an alternative plan of one-to-one contact.

**What About Support for Support Group Leaders?**

Finally, leaders of support groups for assaulted women need to be concerned about their own sources of support.

Here are some areas to consider:

o    get support from your workplace, such as adequate time, facilities and backup.

o    connect with a 24-hour crisis service that you trust, so your group will have outside sources of help.

o    develop a resource person for violent husbands.  Some men will be motivated for treatment by their spouses' action.  Others will be angry and/or threatened by the group.  If you do not feel equipped to deal with these  men, find someone who is.

o    continue to work through your own feelings about wife assault.  Avoid the use of political rhetoric and debates while in the group.

o    establish a support system for those in your location who work in this area.  This will allow you a safe place to deal with your own frustrations and give you a sense that you are not struggling with this issue on your own.

# 8 GROUP MODEL FOR MEN WHO ASSAULT THEIR PARTNERS
by David Currie

## Introduction

One fall evening in September 1980, a group of men gathered together to meet for the first time. They came from all income levels, job categories and educational backgrounds. They were coming together to form the first group of its kind in central or eastern Canada.

The problem was wife assault.

Up until this time, assaulted women were being seen, but there was little or no contact with their partners. A large number of assaulted women were either remaining with, or returning to, abusive partners. These women initiated the men's program themselves by asking that some sort of intervention be provided for their partners.

The program was set up to provide men with an opportunity to stop their violent behaviour. It has been found that approximately 65 to 70% of the men who complete the program end the physical violence towards their partners. At the four-month follow up point, this number is about 60%.

Common statements made by group members after the program is finished:

o    I wish I could have been involved with something like this five years ago. My life has changed in major ways.

o    I used to think my wife was responsible for the violence. Now I realize that I am and that I can change that.

o    If violent men out there would only realize that they could get so much out of a group like this.

This chapter is a compilation of information that describes the group program including the various therapeutic components involved.

## Group Treatment Model -- Theoretical Considerations

Over the past few years, a number of group models have evolved to offer treatment to men. Although there are many similarities between the various programs, there are differences in format (such as cognitive restructuring, consciousness raising, relaxation training) as well as differences in structure (i.e., length, open or closed, or cycles).[1]

The model for this program is psychoeducational. At times there is specific information provided to the men (such as definitions and forms of violence, male/female role stereotyping). At other times, the emphasis is on changing the attitudes held toward themselves and women that contribute to violent behaviour. Emphasis is placed on taking control and responsibility of themselves. This is done through an increase in self-awareness. The support provided by the other group members is seen as an essential contributor towards growth. This group model is an adaptation of the consciousness-raising model that came out of the feminist movement.

In order to design and implement a program to work with men who assault their partners, it is essential to have a clear understanding or working model that attempts to explain the causes of violence. This is important so that the treatment variables are specifically geared to address these underlying causes. To illustrate, if one thought men assault their wives due to a biochemical disturbance in their bodies, drugs would be the treatment of choice.

The Causes of Violence

To understand the reasons men assault their wives requires consideration of both societal and psychological factors.

Imbedded within our society are a number of attitudes and values held by men towards women which condone the use of violence in marriage. For example the demonstration of anger and aggressiveness in men is highly encouraged, both in the world of sports and as a method of solving problems.

This manner of solving conflict has also been supported in family life, which has long been considered the private domain. This private domain has been an ongoing dilemma for many wives. The use of violence by a husband against his wife has long been considered a legitimate form of behaviour as shown, historically, by the lack of measures to deter or stop such behaviour (e.g., police or court intervention or an effective community response).

A scene from a television movie depicts a woman being struck in a bar by a man. Another man yells out, "Hey, you can't hit a woman who's not your wife!"

---

[1] For a description of the philosophy and structure of Canadian programs, the reader is referred to James Browning, Ph.D., Stopping the Violence: Canadian Programmes for Assaultive Men, published by The National Clearinghouse on Family Violence, Health and Welfare Canada, 1984.

Many excuses or myths are propagated to explain why a man is violent towards his wife, such as alcoholism, unemployment or stress brought about by some other circumstances. It is important to consider, though, that the target for these outbursts is frequently only his wife. This being the case, the reason a man's partner is the target is that this kind of behaviour towards her is more tolerated on a social level than similar behaviour to a supervisor, colleague or stranger. This phenomenon illustrates the socially imbedded attitudes that discriminate against and devalue a woman, particularly a woman in the role of wife.

## Psychological Profile

In order to understand more fully men who assault their partners, it is necessary to examine their psychological makeup. Generally speaking there are four main characteristics of men who assault their partners.

### 1. The externalization of blame and minimization of their violent behaviour

Most of the men I have come into contact with see the causes of their violence as located outside of themselves.

> The only reason I hit her was because she was arguing
> with me and wouldn't listen to me.

> I told her to be home by 6 o'clock. If she had been
> home on time, I wouldn't have struck her.

> I had been drinking that night I guess I had too much.

In addition, there is a tendency to minimize and/or deny the frequency and severity of the violence.

> I'm not like those other guys who really beat up their
> wife. I just shoved her a couple of times.

> I've only slapped her twice in the past year.

One of the reasons it is so important to involve the spouse at some point early in the assessment phase is that she will be more capable of accurately describing what actually took place. In the first example above, the man failed to mention that when he shoved her, her head went back and struck a wall, giving her a mild concussion. In the second example, besides the slapping on numerous occasions, the woman was punched in the face on one occasion and required medical attention for a few days in a hospital.

## 2.    Dependency

Many of the men I come into contact with exhibit excessive dependency needs in their primary relationships. This is demonstrated by frequently being preoccupied with their partners' whereabouts and activities. There is a heightened sensitivity to loss and separation; the man's coping abilities become severely strained if his wife leaves the home.

> She left three days ago. I can't stop thinking about her.
> I've been driving around for hours looking for her.
> What's the use in going on without her. I've stopped
> eating, I can't sleep and I can't go to work.

The inability to separate themselves from their partner psychologically is understood on a developmental framework of separation-individuation as an inability to differentiate themselves from their partner. This being so, they are unable to experience themselves and their partners as two separate individuals. When the partner is experienced as an extension of themselves, any attempt for the man to control his partner could also be understood as an attempt to control himself.

This psychological state is also encouraged by social conditioning in marriage that sees "the two join together as one" and the "one" is usually **him**. Historically women were considered property chattels. This attitude is still prevalent with many people today. The glorification of a state of marriage that sees both husband and wife thinking and feeling alike has added further depth to this struggle.

## 3.    Rigid definitions of masculinity and femininity

The majority of men I have worked with adhere to traditional views regarding male and female role behaviours. Such rigid adherence to role behaviours creates stress and isolation. There is the stress that occurs in relation to role performance where role performance is taken as an indicator of their self-worth and often forms the basis for their self-esteem.

The isolation comes from self-imposed limits that in the case of men mean emotional isolation from others.

> I provide well financially for my wife and kids but I'd
> like to have a best friend and I don't feel like I do. I
> don't know how to talk about what I feel.

Preoccupations with performance, controls and getting ahead overshadow and undermine the possibility of a satisfying emotional relationship with his partner.

4.    **Low Self-Esteem**

The men I have worked with have thought and felt a lot of things (e.g., fear, confusion, panic, depression, anger), but have rarely felt good about striking their partners.   Although these men often present themselves as angry and blaming towards their partners, underneath this "external presentation" they felt guilty, remorseful, inadequate and out of control.

Continual instances of violence toward their partner only serve to erode further an already negative self-image.  These men may often feel desperate but would rarely say so, for to admit this would be to move outside the realm of accepted male behaviours.  Anger and depression are often the result when a wife has left.  Ironically, the most important part of the man's life has fallen apart and he feels at a loss for solutions.

## Screening

The screening process is an essential component of the group program.  Besides providing assessment information on the family, it covers safety and protection issues concerning the victim, as well as beginning the engagement process of getting the man involved in treatment.

In the initial stage of treatment, it is important to have contact with both the man and his partner.  There should be one assessment session with the partner and one with the man.  (The type of questions asked can be found in Exhibit 1 at the end of this chapter.)  Men tend to minimize the extent of the violence.  An accurate portrayal of what happened can only be determined by having contact with both parties.

To maximize the safety of the woman, the opportunity to meet with her alone allows for not just an assessment of the past and present circumstances, but an opportunity to discuss safety and protection measures that she may be unfamiliar with. Furthermore, I discuss with her the format of the men's group program, so that she understands what it is that her partner is entering into.  I explain that one of the ground rules is that she can call me if at any time she is in doubt as to what is taking place in the program.

## Assessment

The man sets the screening process into action by making the first phone call to initiate counselling.  Most men call because they feel fearful that part of their lives is out of control and they are unsure of how to straighten things out.  An actual or threatened separation by their partners is what brings most men into treatment in the first place.

At the time of the first call by the man, an appointment for an assessment session will be set up with him, after a brief telephone discussion concerning when violence last took place; how frequently it has occurred; and what the potential is for further violence from his point of view.

The assessment interview is set up as soon as possible after his initial phone contact. Often the man is feeling in crisis at the time of his call and he will be easier to engage in treatment if the contact is immediate. Also, there is no contact with the victim at this point, so her safety may continue to be in jeopardy. At the time of the first session he is informed that part of the program involves the group leader having contact with the partners of the men involved.

The screening process is an important time to attempt to engage the man in ongoing counselling. It is important that he feel welcome, accepted and understood by the group leader. We must remember that most men find reaching out for counselling at best a difficult step to take and so need to be well supported when they do so.

Another important aspect of the screening process is to assess the nature of the man's motivation. Most men, at the point of initial contact, are motivated to change because of some external circumstance (e.g., their wife is threatening to leave or she has left and refuses to return until he stops being violent with her). The man is beginning to realize that he has a problem in his marriage, even though he may hold his wife responsible for the problem.

During the assessment, a man would be encouraged to seek individual counselling, either prior to or at the same time as the group sessions, if he was in an extreme state of crisis.

A man would be excluded from group membership if he were seen to possess any psychiatric symptoms that would interfere with the group process. Also, a man with a serious alcohol problem would be referred to an alcoholism treatment program for completion prior to attending this group.

## Ground Rules

The screening is also to familiarize the man with why the group program was set up and what the format is. If the man has never been in counselling before, he may be unfamiliar with what is expected of him in the program. He may particularly be unsure about what the role of the group leader is. This would be found in situations where a man thinks he is joining a series of lectures or a course on what to do to stop being violent. Although the group process may resemble this from time to time, it is not a classroom-type experience.

This is clarified at the time of intake. The men are told that the greater their motivation to change their behaviour and the more active their involvement in the group, the greater will be the results of the program for them.

The program's attendance expectations are outlined. The men must be able to attend eight of the ten sessions and must promise to attend the full session each week (i.e., they must not arrive late or leave early). If factors such as shift work interfere with regular group involvement, alternatives such as individual sessions are discussed.

## Safety and Protection of Partner

At the end of the screening, the man, if accepted, is given the starting date of the group. He is told that the group leader will be in contact with his partner as part of the assessment and screening. He is also told the reasons for contacting his partner and that she will be contacted by the group leader if at any point in the group program her safety is considered to be in jeopardy. This is done because the safety and protection of the victim are always held to be of utmost importance.

Finally, the man is shown a copy of the written agreement he signs in order to be a group member (see Exhibit 2). He takes this contract home to look it over and brings it back for signing at the end of the first group session.

## Content of Sessions

The content of the program was specifically chosen to reflect and be consistent with the beliefs and assumptions about the causes of violence. Thus, the psychological needs of the men who batter are balanced with the need to address the social issues.

Given the above, a list of content items is presented in chart form, including an approximate time frame for when they are addressed in the group. A description of each item, along with a rationale for its use, follows.

---

## GROUP SESSIONS

---

| 1 2 3 | 4 5 6 7 8 | 9 10 |
|---|---|---|
| 1. Introductions | 9. Films | 13. Termination |
| 2. Joining | 10. Personal time | 14. Evaluation |
| 3. Contracting | 11. Male/female roles | 15. Future planning |
| 4. Questions | 12. Dependency chart | |
| 5. Anger log* | | |
| 6. Pre-violence cues | | |
| 7. Alternatives | | |
| 8. Check-in/check-out* | | |

---

1.   Introductions

Introductions occur during the early part of the first group meeting. Each member introduces himself to the group and gives a description of why he joined the group, what his family circumstances are, how he found out about the group and what his personal goals are for being in the group.

The purpose of this exercise is to begin to reduce isolation. The building of group cohesion and identification with the group starts through this sort of interaction. The members are becoming familiar with each other and their respective circumstances.

2.   Joining

Joining is the term that best describes the way a leader attempts to engage the members in the treatment process. The leader creates an atmosphere of caring and acceptance while still maintaining that their violent behaviour is unacceptable. It reflects a high degree of respect for the men as people and an awareness of the individual struggles of each member. The joining process is most important in the screening and early stages of the group.

The joining process is concentrated on at great length because members often minimize their problem of violence and so are reluctant to engage in treatment. In addition, members are frequently fearful of any treatment

---

\*   Check-in and Check-out and Anger log are regular parts of the process in each group session.

process since they think that "a man should be able to handle his problems himself." The members often feel humiliated or embarrassed by coming for counselling in the first place.

### 3.  Contracting

Contracting takes place at the end of the first group meeting. The men sign an agreement outlining the expectations of them as a group member (such as attendance, honesty, level of participation). A copy of the written agreement can be found in Exhibit 2.

The purpose of the written contract is to formalize their commitment to counselling and to the group in particular. It also serves to structure the crisis they are in and thus is therapeutic. It is a tool to help them be responsible and accountable. It sets limits that they are able to manage and so is a direct example of the immediate building of self-esteem.

The drop off rate for prospective members was reduced substantially when the formalized agreement was instituted. It emphasized the importance of each member making solid commitment for change in his life.

### 4.  Use of Questions to Challenge Stereotypic Belief Systems

Although questions are asked throughout the group sessions, specific questions are asked during the first and second sessions as a way of introducing the topic of violence, and of getting the members to work together therapeutically.

The particular questions asked are: What is violence? Where does it come from? How has violence been a problem for the members themselves? Who's responsible for violence? What are the benefits of becoming non-violent? What will be the costs of not changing?

The purpose of asking these questions in this particular fashion is to facilitate the members' involvement in their own change process. In this respect, the therapeutic outcome will be much greater than if the men had all these questions answered for them. It is an attempt to have the men begin to want to change for their own sakes. The questions are asked in a way that doesn't challenge their responses yet but serves to have the members begin to share their ideas and feelings about themselves and question some of the ideas they have held up until this point in time.

### 5.  Anger Log

A weekly log book of situations arousing anger is explained to all members during the first night and is used throughout the group as a weekly exercise. The anger log can be found in Exhibit 3. A copy of the anger log is given to each member and its purpose and method are explained. Members are required to fill out the anger log, where applicable, during the week and then one or two examples are used near the start of each group session.

The purpose of the anger log is to have the members begin to identify feelings of anger and what circumstances led to their feeling this way; they then begin to look at ways that they increased or decreased the level of anger that they were feeling.

This exercise helps members gain control over the thoughts and feelings they had while they were angry. One member stated, "I took this sheet with me to work last week so I could look it over when I felt anger towards my boss. It really helped."

## 6. Pre-Violence Cues

In this exercise, usually done on the second group night, the members think back over previous incidents of violence and try to identify the visual, auditory and emotional signs or signals that were present just prior to the violent incident. The members are asked to remember what they saw at the time, what they remember hearing and what they recall feeling.

The purpose of this exercise is to have members begin to identify potentially violent situations before they get out of control. Once out of control, there is little awareness of what takes place or how to get back in control. If the situation doesn't get to the point of being out of control, then an alternative to the violent response can more easily be selected. In order for this to happen, an increased awareness of the buildup signs and signals is needed.

One member remarked at the start of the exercise, "I didn't know I was going to be violent, it just all of a sudden happened and I was out of control." One week after doing the exercise, he reported back: "Last Sunday my wife and I were out with the kids. I began to feel and see some of the signs which told me I was **starting** to get out of control. I quickly decided to go for a walk by myself and everything was fine when I returned."

## 7. Alternatives

Closely related in timing with the previolence cues exercise is a discussion that often occurs in the second session about alternatives to the violent response. The members are asked by the group leader to begin to think of alternatives that they have either tried in the past or could think of trying.

Again here, the onus is on the members themselves to come up with alternatives and the group leader to facilitate this process. If any member finds it difficult to think of any alternatives or has reasons why various alternatives wouldn't work for him, the group members will challenge the member, perhaps with some assistance or modelling from the group leader.

8.   Check-In/Check-Out

A process of check-in and check-out begins on the first session and runs throughout the group.  The check-in involves each member briefly describing what kind of a week he has had, along with a statement as to how he is feeling. The check-out involves each member briefly describing what they thought of the group session.  The group leader also takes part in this exercise for role-modelling purposes.

The purpose of the exercise is to further decrease the isolation experienced by members and facilitate their relating to each other on an emotional level.  This serves to increase group cohesion and therefore the therapeutic impact of the group program.  It also allows the leaders and members to monitor the presence of ongoing violence or crisis potential of each member on a weekly basis.  Incidents of violence identified during this exercise are taken seriously and given priority in the evening's discussion.

9.   Films

Audio-visual films have been used to generate a discussion about certain topics as well as providing an alternative mode of covering certain material with the members.

For example, one reason why men assault their wives is because of a particular set of attitudes that they hold towards women and values that serve to condone wife assault.  It is believed that a change in these attitudes will be reflected in a change in behaviour by these men towards their partners.  The film titled "To Have and To Hold" describes a men's counselling service in Boston for men who are batterers.  The film examines the underlying attitudes and values that men hold towards women.  The film gives the group members the same message as they've already discussed in earlier parts of the group. This serves to develop an awareness of the social context within which violence occurs, to reduce isolation and the feeling of being alone and to develop an awareness of the extent of the problem.

Other films used are:  "Shifting Gears"; "Killing Us Softly"; and "Battered Women:  Violence Behind Closed Doors."[2]

---

[2]   These films are available through the Family Violence Prevention Program (refer to Appendix F).

### 10. Personal Time

This is time, particularly during the middle phase of the group, when the members are encouraged to share. This provides an opportunity for the man to receive feedback from other members concerning how he handled whatever situation he chose to talk about. The time period also allows for discussing any ongoing incidents of violence that occurred during the previous week. There is often much discussion and challenging amongst members during these periods. Essentially, then, it is a time for individual problem-solving with group feedback and support.

### 11. Male/Female Roles

A discussion of male/female role expectations is seen as an important component of the middle phase of the group. The exercise involves placing the terms male and female at the top of a flipchart. Then members are asked to provide terms to characterize either side. What gets generated are two long lists of terms that are very mixed in their descriptions and represent the views and attitudes of the men towards each sex. The same exercise is done for the terms "husband" and "wife."

The purpose of the exercise is to demonstrate that sex-role descriptions are assigned and not biologically inherited. This is clearly demonstrated by the many contradictions expressed (e.g., women are strong/weak). Such an exercise serves to generate much discussion among members as they begin to understand more clearly how rigid role expectations contribute to violence, as well as how they can undermine a person's self-esteem and self-image.

As a result of this exercise, the men begin to see how they themselves have been victims of male sex-role stereotyping, which has served to restrict some important aspects of their lives, particularly in the area of emotional life.

> I always wanted my wife to be my best friend but I
> could never talk about my feelings. I thought I wouldn't
> be strong if I did that.

### 12. Dependency Chart

Also during the middle phase of the group and as an outgrowth of other discussions concerning sex-role behaviours, the topic of dependency in relationships surfaces. In order to illustrate the idea of healthy versus unhealthy dependency, the following chart is drawn looking at three different relationship styles.

1. 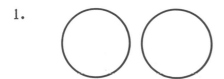 **Independent.** Characterized by distance, no intimacy, no support, loneliness.

2. 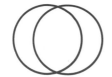 **Dependent.** Characterized by tension, instability, loss of self-control, immobilization, insecurity, need, anxiety, fatigue, little toleration for differences.

3. 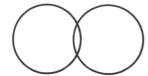 **Interdependent.** Awareness, closeness, variety, respect for differences, movement, want, self-control, friendship.

The men are asked to select which style they think they fit into. Most of them select #2. A discussion ensues then as to how to move from #2 to #3.

The purpose of this exercise is to increase self-awareness as to how the men's frequent preoccupation with their partners' thoughts, feelings and actions leads to further difficulties for both themselves and their partners. It also serves to help reduce the level of dependency that the men have on their partners. This begins to happen as they view themselves as separate individuals from their partners. At the same time, they base more of their self-image and self-esteem in themselves rather than specific role behaviours in relation to their partners.

As the men begin to view their partners more as separate individuals and less as extensions of themselves, the quality of their relationships improve and their self-esteem rises.

13. Termination Discussion

The issue of termination should be raised in the second-last session by the group leader if one of the group members hasn't already raised it. This allows two sessions for the group members to talk about their thoughts and feelings about the group ending. This is important so that the members identify and learn to deal with their feelings, which are often quite intense at this stage of the group.

As part of the termination discussion, each member talks about the progress he thinks he has made in the group and how the group experience has helped him to change. Feedback to each member is given by any member of the group or leader at the time the member is talking of his progress.

The purpose of this discussion is to allow the members enough time to work through their feelings of sadness and loss as the group comes to an end. In addition, it serves the purpose of the men consolidating the changes they've made.

## 14. Evaluation

A verbal and written evaluation is undertaken in the last session. A copy of the written evaluation questionnaire is found in Exhibit 4. The verbal evaluation is similar to the written one, in that it asks members to comment on their experience of being in the group, what they liked and disliked about the program, what was most useful for them and what they would recommend for future groups. This is important because once again it makes them articulate clearly their thoughts and feelings (both positive and negative) about the group and their involvement in it.

The purpose of the evaluations is to have members look back over the ten-week program and think about the impact of various sessions on their progress. Another important purpose is to gain valuable information in order to constantly refine and improve the group model so as to offer a most effective service.

## 15. Future Planning

This involves each group member examining what growth and change they still have to accomplish. In line with this, further counselling (individual, couple or indeed group sessions) is considered. In addition, each member is asked to identify what he would do in the future when he thought he may be about to be violent again.

The purpose of this exercise is to enable the members to understand that growth and development are ongoing processes and don't stop because the group happens to be over. It also enables each member to plan ahead and be ready with some sort of strategy should he find himself violent or about to be violent in the future.

## Group Processes

In the initial stages of the group (sessions 1 to 3), there is a fair degree of fear, anxiety and lack of trust as the members begin to work together. For most of them, it is the first time they have ever been involved in group counselling and certainly the first time for this purpose. As a result, the members are uncertain about each other and are very interested in the situations of the other members present.

The leaders in the initial phase have a fairly high profile in that most of the nights' activities or discussions are structured by the leaders.

In the middle phase of the group (sessions 4 to 8), the members become much more comfortable in talking with each other. A level of trust and cohesion is built up, to the extent that members begin to confront and challenge each other about some of their ideas or behaviour. This is done in a way that the members seem to feel supported in their attempts to look at themselves. Many of the group members at this point begin to take on a therapist role with other members. This is not only seen as appropriate but is encouraged by the group leaders so that members are better able to learn from each other.

The role of the leaders in this phase of the program is much more low key than the initial phase. The role of facilitators would best describe what the leaders do during these sessions. The leaders keep the group focussed on a relevant topic and introduce films as the need arises. The group is actively working together therapeutically by this point.

In the final phase of the group (sessions 9 and 10), the group members begin to comment on what a short period of time there is left and how they would like to see the group continue.

At this stage in time, the leaders' role takes on a higher profile again as the group goes through the termination phase. An increase in the structure of the sessions is initiated by the group leaders.

## Outcome Measures

The main goal of the group is for members to stop being violent toward their partners. At the evaluation when we ask whether there has been further incidents of violence, we are speaking of verbal abuse, physical abuse or property damage as outlined in this manual. Before entering the program, the problem of being violent is identified, either by the man or his partner. At the end of the group, the outcome for every member is measured by:

A.    His own verbal report of changes that have occurred while he has been involved in the program (including of course the question, "have there been any further violent incidents?").

B.    His partner, who is contacted and asked if there have been any further incidents of violence and whether she has noticed any other changes since her partner has been involved in the group program.

In addition, a follow-up session is held for all members four months after the group ends.  The purpose of the follow-up session is to further assess the effectiveness of the program in terms of the cessation of violence as well as other changes.  As before, both the man and his partner are asked for this information.  The partner is usually contacted by phone.  A copy of the follow up evaluation form can be found in Exhibit 5.

## Evaluation of the Group Program

A.    Advantages

o    The program can be operated in settings where either staffing time and/or financial resources are limited.

o    Ten weeks is an adequate amount of time to enable members to begin making changes, provided that follow-up counselling is available.

o    A ten-week structure is useful for purposes of a demonstration project prior to the establishment of an ongoing program.  It is time limited with a clear structure and content.

o    The group format is an effective mode of intervention for many men.

o    The group format allows for variations in the leaders' styles and expertise.  These variations can be easily accommodated by this structure.

o    The ten-week structure can be easily modified into an ongoing program, as some programs presently operate.

B.    Disadvantages

o    The ten-week structure doesn't allow for the unique needs of the individual members.  A member finishes his contact with the program because it is finished, as opposed to his ending because he has met the goals of the group or his own individual goals.

o    The startup time and energy required of group leaders is significant.  A ten-week structure means this has to be repeated each time a new group gets underway.

o    If the program is not of an ongoing nature, the more advanced members (found in ongoing programs) aren't present to help as resources with new members.

o    The amount of stress on a group leader is much greater in a ten-week structure; therefore a co-leadership model is highly preferable.  This involves doubling staff time.

o    If the program is not run on an ongoing basis, the number of men who complete the program in a year is significantly less than with an ongoing structure.

o    If there is not an ongoing program, men are put on a waiting list. For maximum effect, they should move into treatment while in crisis and their motivation for change is high.

C.    Recommendations

o    It is essential that treatment programs for men not operate in isolation in the community. In order to provide a higher profile and be part of a community of resources to families where wife assault is occurring, the program needs to be part of a comprehensive service network. This program should only be set up in conjunction with services to women and children and not before them.

o    A research component is essential for the ongoing clinical development and funding of programs for men. Through research, a demonstrated effectiveness for this type of program is possible.

o    Burnout can be a serious problem in this program area. This danger can be minimized by an organization's demonstrated support for such a program. Co-leadership also helps to reduce the threat of burnout. Being part of a comprehensive service network to wife-assault families provides support not just to the families served, but also to the service providers.

o    Programs of this sort should not be competing for basic funds required for the provision of services to assaulted women and their children. This is particularly true for women's shelters as well as support groups for assaulted women.

**Personal Reflections**

The satisfactions in this area of my work came quickly as the first group program began to unfold. As we all worked together, learning from each other, I began to see very clearly the internal pain, constraint and fear that these men had imposed on their lives. They were attempting to live up to an image of maleness to which they had been introduced to years earlier, and in many respects they were victims themselves of traditional male socialization.

Under an external veneer of control and competence lurked the troubling feelings of fear, inadequacy and lack of self-worth. The group work in part has been an attempt to help these men build and rebuild their internal thoughts and feelings about themselves, so that they can live more constructive and satisfying lives with others, particularly with their partners.

I have found working with these men particularly satisfying, in that I also have grown up male with all the male role conditioning and stereotyping that goes with it. I too have struggled with, and still struggle with, my "male" attitudes towards myself and towards women.

I have found the group program immensely satisfying. How do you get someone to involve themselves in a change process that they are threatened by and yet can hold so much promise for them and their future? This has been the challenge.

It is exciting to work past the external presentation to the rich world inside of men whose depth is so often underdeveloped. To watch them grow and develop their potentials has been a great reward!

Working in isolation from others has been particularly stressful. Solid and demonstrable support from colleagues is an essential ingredient. Also stressful at times has been a feeling of responsibility to facilitate a particularly resistant man into the change process, knowing that if he doesn't involve himself, his present or future partner is in great danger.

Is it worth it? I'm still involved in the issue and plan to remain so. I know that because of the efforts and interest of all men's group leaders, and the men themselves, we will make a significant contribution to the reduction of wife assault.

I think that men must also model non-violent behaviour for other men and challenge the status quo. In doing so, we will become an important part of a network that will eventually end violence against women.

We should not expect women to end male violence. Women have been the victims of male violence for far too long now. It is a time for change. My ongoing involvement in this area as a group leader, a therapist and workshop leader has been my way of trying to contribute to the reduction of social inequality that exists for women.

## Exhibit 1   Screening Questionnaire

1.  How long have you been married or in a significant relationship?

    How long have you known your partner?

    How old are you and your partner?

2.  Are there any children in the relationship?  What are their sexes and ages?

3.  Please give a description of the violence that presently occurs in the relationship.

    When was the last incident?

    In what ways were you violent towards your partner?  Specify.

    How frequently have you been violent?

    Has your partner ever required medical attention for injuries due to a violent incident?

    Have the police ever been called in?

    Have assault charges ever been laid?

    Has there ever been any damage to property or possessions?

    Have you ever been violent towards the children?

4.  Have you ever been violent in previous relationships with women?

    If so, please describe and specify.

5.  Are you violent outside of your primary relationship?

    If so, please describe and specify.

6.  What do you think is the cause of your violent behaviour?

7.  Please describe your present occupation and work history.

8.  Is there any alcohol use at the time of the violence?

    If yes, what is the quantity and frequency of the drinking behaviour?

    Have you ever assaulted your partner without having had anything to drink?

    Do you think you have a drinking problem?

9.  Who was in your family of origin?

    Did you ever see your father hitting your mother?

    Did you ever know that he did hit her?

    Were you ever abused or severely punished by your parents?

    What do you think was the cause of the violence in your family of origin?

10.  Have you ever sought counselling before?
     What was the outcome?

11.  How did you learn about this program?

12.  Why are you interested in this group?

13.  What are you wanting to accomplish by being in this group?

## Exhibit 2  Men's Group Agreement

I want to join the men's group concerning violence.  The goal of the group is to stop being violent towards my partner.

Participation in the group involves talking about myself and hearing feedback from others, as well as listening to others and giving feedback.  This information and feedback sharing is done to assist all group members in being successful in achieving the group goals.

There are no smoking, drugs or alcohol during group.  Intoxicated or high individuals should not attend groups.

The group begins and ends on time.  If you are more than ten minutes late, do not come since this will interrupt the group.

If you cannot attend, call the leader and leave a message.  Your absence should be explained to the group at the next meeting to maintain group solidarity.

In being a group member, I agree to accept the responsibility to:

A.   attend all sessions regularly and on time;

B.   work on my commitment to stop using violent behaviour;

C.   begin to learn alternative ways of handling stress and frustration;

D.   begin to identify sexist behaviour and attitudes in myself and my fellow group members;

E.   use the group time to discuss any personal situations that I would like to share;

F.   provide constructive feedback to other members;

G.   assist other members by pointing out how some of their attitudes or ideas may be either constructive or destructive.


Signature: _____

EXHIBIT 3

THE ANGER LOG

| TRIGGER | LEVEL OF ANGER | ANGER UP SELF TALK | ANGER DOWN SELF TALK |
|---|---|---|---|
| | | | |

* Taken from Anne L. Ganley, Ph. D.  Court-Mandated Counselling For Men Who Batter: A Three-Day Workshop For Mental Health Professionals. Participant's Manual.

**Exhibit 4   Group Evaluation**

What aspects were most helpful to you in the group experience?

What aspects were least helpful to you in the group experience?

What are things you would have liked to get out of the group but didn't?

If you have had individual counselling, how did the group experience differ?

Did you have sufficient opportunity to discuss the things that were bothering you in the group?   Yes _____ No _____.   If no, why?

Would you have preferred more or less direction from the counsellor?
Explain.

Did you feel that the topics discussed in the group sessions were generally related to your own problems?

We would like your comments on how the leadership was set in the group.

Do you have any suggestions for future groups of this sort?

Any further comments.

**Exhibit 5   Follow Up Evaluation**

1.   Have there been any violent incidents since the group ended?

2.   Did you handle it any differently than you might have before the group? Describe how.

3.   How have you handled being angry since the last group session?

4.   How is this different than before the group?

5.   Has your participation in the group changed the way you think about violence?

6.   Do you think you need any further help with violence or any other aspect of your life?

7.   Are you presently in contact with your partner?

8.   Would you describe that relationship as better, worse or the same as before the group?

9.   In looking back now, what was the most useful part of the group program for you?

10.   What did you learn in the group that you still use in your day-to-day life?

11.   Do your think this group program should be offered to other men?

12.   Do you have any suggestions for encouraging other men to participate in this kind of program?

13.   What changes would you suggest to make it more effective?

14.   Would you be willing to be involved in ongoing aspects of this program (such as media requests; outreach to other men; public education)?

15.   What would you do if you were violent again or felt you might be?

16.   What plans do you have for continuing to improve the quality of your life?

# 9  A PRELIMINARY MODEL FOR GROUP WORK WITH CHILDREN

Group work with children from wife assault families is still a relatively new area. This chapter is an attempt to draw together some of my own experience while also drawing on the work of others in the field, primarily child care workers in transition houses. There is no definitive group model for children. For this reason, the following material should be viewed as a foundation upon which to build your own ideas and to stimulate your own thinking. This chapter answers many of the most commonly asked questions about group work with children from wife-assault families.*

## Why is a group for children important?

Children need the same kind of support and advocacy that their parents need. They need to know they are not alone with this problem. Becoming a member of a group lessens the isolation children feel. By creating a safe place for children to talk about their experiences, a leader models an alternative to the secrecy surrounding their home lives. Meeting other children in the same position lessens their feelings of guilt and self-blame. It is much easier to believe it's not your fault if you have a chance to meet other "normal" children who are not to blame either. The group offers a safe atmosphere to express their fears and confusion about their situation and to validate their experiences. The group also creates an opportunity to unlearn destructive myths and find more effective problem-solving methods than the ones they are familiar with. Most importantly, the group is a special place where children are believed, respected and listened to.

## What does a group leader need to know before starting a group for children?

Although a group leader does not have to be a child specialist, a general understanding of the following issues is essential to leading a children's program. A group leader must:

---

*    I am grateful to Rhonda Freeman, Coordinator of the Families In Transition program of the Family Service Association of Metropolitan Toronto, for the opportunity to participate in her research program on children from separated and divorced families. Her knowledge and expertise have taught me volumes about doing group work with children.

o    have a clear understanding of wife assault and its effects on all members of the family.

o    understand the impact of violence on children.

o    be familiar with the signs and symptoms of child abuse and its forms.

o    be familiar with methods of handling suspected cases of child abuse and potential disclosures that may occur during the group program.

o    have a general understanding of child development theory and child management skills.

o    have realistic expectations of children at different ages and stages.

o    be familiar with community resources for children in case you need to refer a child for specialized help, such as play therapy, speech therapy or educational tutoring.

o    have an empathetic understanding of the stressful demands placed on a parent and the complexity of the parenting role.

o    understand the impact of sex-role stereotyping on children.

o    understand the effects of separation and divorce on children.

o    understand the responsibilities of a child advocate.

**What are the goals of the children's group?**

All of the group goals are based on the underlying philosophy presented throughout this manual: no person has a **right** to assault you and no person ever **deserves** to be assaulted!  An ongoing theme initiated early in the group process and reinforced throughout the program is building a child's sense of self-worth and value as a special person.*  The child is hailed as the **expert** whose opinion is the most important aspect of the whole program.

The group goals include:

o    creating a safe atmosphere for children to talk about themselves and their situations.  **Safety is paramount.**

o    providing factual information about wife assault and child abuse so children can unlearn destructive myths.

o    learning to identify and express a range of feelings in a constructive way, with special emphasis on expressing anger non-violently.

o    exploring alternative role models to the familiar, but often oppressive, ones the children already know.

---

*    Refer to the books by Maureen Miller and Jack Canfield in the children's bibliography at the end of chapter 6 for an excellent variety of esteem-building exercises that are easily adaptable for any children's program.

o        enhancing children's feelings of self-esteem and trust.

o        increasing children's personal support systems.

o        increasing children's awareness of their right and responsibilities and realistic ways of dealing with them.

o        alleviating children's sense of responsibility for parental problems.

o        helping children sort out the ambivalent feelings they may have towards their parents.

o        helping children develop alternative program-solving skills and creating opportunities to practice them in the group.

### Where do the group referrals come from?

If you work in an agency setting, most referrals will initially come from your own caseload. As your interest in the area becomes known, referrals will likely be initiated by your co-workers, particularly if they are sensitized to the issue. The referrals ultimately will be expanded into the community. Shelters and women's crisis centres are an excellent source of referrals. Your credibility as a group leader and your sensitivity to the issues must be established _prior_ to expecting referrals from these sources. Eventually, referrals tend to come from word of mouth through clients and informed service providers.

### What role do mothers play?

My involvement with children first began at the request of their mothers. Once many of the assaulted women had worked through their own issues, usually in a group context, they would return to me requesting assistance with their children.

Initially, I believed that any service that improved the well-being of the mother would indirectly benefit the children. While this belief still holds, it does not suffice. Children need their own special place and mothers need a special time to participate in a child-focussed program.

Ideally, women should first have participated in a group program focussed on their own needs. Once the goals of that program have been achieved, they are freer to address their children's needs. If this is not possible, a mothers' group must be formed to try and balance her needs with those of her children. It is unrealistic to expect a mother to participate in a solely child-focussed program if she has never had the opportunity to focus on herself.

### What are the purposes of a mothers' group?

1.    To sensitize mothers to the impact of violence on their children.

2. To provide nonviolent alternatives to disciplining children and information on general child-management techniques.

3. To help them understand the connection between wife assault and child abuse.

4. To help mothers differentiate between the normal developmental needs of children and those that are problematic.

5. To help mothers recognize that their children are in crisis and to help them empathize with their children's feelings.

6. To support mothers in their search for more meaningful communication with their children.

7. To recognize the difficulty of parenting and to support them in that role.

8. To sensitize mothers to the impact of separation and divorce on their children.

9. To sensitize mothers to the impact of sex-role stereotyping on their children.

The mothers' group is run in conjunction with the children's group. For example, the children's group runs from 4:30 to 6:00 p.m. and the mothers' group runs from 7:00 to 9:00 p.m. Child care should be provided or babysitting costs subsidized. Confidentiality is maintained at all times, except when the leader suspects a child is in some kind of danger. Then both the mother and the child welfare authorities must be informed. It would be important for the group leader to help the child talk to the mother about the problem prior to notifying child welfare authorities. If this process is incorporated into the group rules, all the children will be familiar with it and will not feel betrayed if protective actions must be taken. Children need to be reassured continually that their safety is a priority and that the group leaders will take this responsibility seriously. Although individual comments may not be divulged from the children's group, general feedback about children's concerns and reactions is highly encouraged. One group even wrote a collective letter to their Moms to read at the parents' group as a way of communicating their concerns. It was a huge success.

**What information do you need to obtain from the mother?**

In a screening interview with the child's mother it is important to develop as full a picture as possible of her concerns regarding her children. Hopefully, you will already have a fairly clear picture of each family member's situation. (Refer back to sections of this manual on assessment with each family member.)  This meeting is to gain specifics on each individual child's reactions to the violence.  Find out:

o      What the children know about their parents' situation.

o      What exposure the children have had to the violence.

o      Specific details of children's reactions to the situation (for example, physical symptoms, behavioural problems, school problems).

o      What the parental plan is to deal with the violence (for example, separation, group counselling, legal actions).

o      What kind of relationship each parent has with the child.

o      What custody and access arrangements exist and how well they work (if separated).

o      What discipline is used and how effective she finds her methods.

o      What her relationship is like with her partner and the impact it has on the children.

**What role do fathers play?**

Although fathers have not played a primary role in this child-focussed program, their willingness to do so would be an asset.  Wherever possible, if both the children and their mothers are in agreement, it would be useful to find out the same details from the father as from the mother, especially if he is still an active presence in the children's lives.  The gathering of this information takes place in an individual interview with the father and gives the group leader the opportunity to engage him in the counselling process if he has not yet been motivated to change his behaviour.

A fathers' group, modelled after the mothers' group, might be an additional strategy to experiment with, if there are enough fathers available to form a group.  It would probably be necessary for these men to already have participated in the men's group. If they have not yet assumed full responsibility for their violent behaviour, they would not likely have the capacity to empathize with their children's feelings or the ability to put their children's needs ahead of their own needs.

It is always in the children's best interest for the group leader to attempt to help the man who assaults his wife to take responsibility for his violent behaviour and to understand the impact of his violent behaviour on his children.

Assessments from other sources, such as the child-care worker in the shelter, the child's teacher, the family doctor and/or the referring agent, might also be helpful in developing a clear picture of the child's situation.

**How should the child be introduced to the group program?**

In a joint interview with the child and the mother, the mother is given the opportunity to explain the program to her child and to outline her reasons for wanting her child to participate in the group. Because this takes place in the leader's presence, it allows for the clarification of information and gives an opportunity for observing the interaction between the mother and her child. It is important to establish the mother's authority from the very beginning. This approach minimizes the possibility of the group leader being over-idealized by the child and avoids the group leader being placed in a competitive stance with the mother.

**Can any child join the group?**

Yes. The only exception is a severely disturbed child who would not be able to concentrate in a group atmosphere. This child might benefit from special individual attention prior to enrolling in a group program. It is also important to note that this group program is not designed to deal specifically with children who have been sexually abused. These children will require special assistance from experienced workers in the field of child sexual abuse in addition to this program.* Children who act out or are disruptive are typical of this population, so to rule them out would defeat your purpose. Clear ground rules must be established and followed to deal with discipline problems. The group is an ideal setting for providing live examples of non-violent methods of discipline. Children's cooperation is encouraged in deciding fair consequences for unacceptable behaviours.

**What is a typical group format?**

Each session begins with a formal snack time lasting from ten to fifteen minutes. Fresh fruit, vegetables, crackers and juice are suggested and enjoyed by the children. Healthy snacks are encouraged as sugar treats may only heighten the hyperactivity in the group.

The session then moves to a check-in, where children are encouraged to introduce themselves individually, report back on their homework (if assigned),comment on their safety at home and comment on any relevant developments since the last session. **Priority is always given to any child**

---

\*    Contact the Ontario Centre for the Prevention of Child Abuse for
      information on sexual abuse programs for children (See Appendix F).

**perceived to be in crisis.**

Individual problem-solving is built into each session. For example, if one child reports an incident with his Dad where the child was being persuaded to divulge his Mom's whereabouts, the group leaders might schedule special time on the agenda to deal with that problem.

After the check-in, the topic is introduced. Individual time is always balanced with the time needed for the topic discussion. Movement to each should be flexible and based on the members' needs.

As each session reaches the end, closure should be achieved. One method of obtaining closure is to encourage the children to review what they have learned in the group thus far. For example, "Who remembers the rules about your body that we learned in last week's session?" It is important to build on each previous week's learning. Repetition is a powerful tool, especially with children. Reviewing previous sessions also serves as a reminder of the time-limited nature of the group. For example, "We've had four sessions already, how many do we have left?" Since fear of separation is a major therapeutic issue with these children, it is imperative that they have the opportunity to successfully experience a positive ending in their lives. The group prepares them for this experience.

If any child has had a strong emotional response to the content in the session, then extra time should be taken to help that child resolve the crisis before the session ends. No child should leave the group in too vulnerable a position.

### What about . . .?

#### Ages of children

Ideally, children should be separated according to their ages and stages of development. This means the most typical age divisions would be:

#### Ages

| | | |
|---|---|---|
| 3 to 6 years | - | Pre-school group |
| 7 to 12 years | - | Latency group |
| 13 or more years | - | Adolescent group |

Most times this is not possible because of lack of numbers or shortage of staffing. I have run groups with children ranging in age from four up to thirteen within the same program. The success of the age and stage mix will largely depend on the children's personalities and the leader's skill at dealing with age-related concerns. Unlike other child-activity programs, age and stage are not the critical issues in this program. Regardless of the child's age or ability, all children from wife-assault homes need to get certain information simply because they are in that kind of home. The focus is thus an educational one where children are given access to necessary information in ways they can understand. Flexibility is the key. However, the less diversity in age and ability there is in the same group, the easier the tasks are for the leaders.

For most children, this type of group is all they will need. But as with their parents, some children will need additional assistance outside of the group. For these children, consideration of their age and stage would be essential in tailoring a plan of action to meet their individual needs.

## Number of children

The ideal number is from eight to twelve. However, a group can be run with as few as three or four children.

## Structure

The group sessions generally run for 1½ hours on a weekly basis. Younger children may need breaks, whereas adolescents can usually benefit from longer programs (e.g., 2 hours). Each cycle lasts for six sessions and membership is closed after the second session. Old members can rejoin the next cycle if they want to. Children from previous cycles tend to act as resource persons and role models for newer members.

## Leadership

A male and female leading team is the ideal. This combination offers alternative role-modelling to traditional sex-role socialization. Each co-leader must agree with the group philosophy. It is an asset if at least one of the co-leaders is a parent.

It is **not** necessary for the same leaders to run both the mother's group and the children's group, although that has been my experience and it was quite effective. If different leaders run each group ongoing, regular communication is essential.

## Physical space

An ideal space is one where the room has been cleared of all furniture and only pillows remain. Children can sit on the pillows and move them quickly for easy physical movement. This atmosphere is less stressful for the leaders as they will not have to spend their time controlling what the children do with furniture, breakables, and so on. Leaders will not have to be so authoritarian if the physical space is designed to accommodate the children's needs. The worst thing that can happen, and likely will, is pillow fights. This kind of physical space also minimizes the distractions for the children.

## Siblings

There is no definite stance on the issue of siblings in the same group. More importantly, each situation should be individually assessed. If the sibs have a history of antagonism, separate groups for each might be more constructive. If they have a positive rapport, their mutual presence might be an asset for the group. It is important to experiment with different combinations.

## Films

All films in this program should be available through your local public library.

**What are the group rules?**

o      We are all in this group for the same reason. Everyone comes from a home where their Dads hit their Moms.

o      Anything you say will be believed.

o      Hurting someone with words or hands is not permitted.

o      Everyone must try their very best to listen when a member is talking. It is an important way to show respect to each other.

o      It's okay to ask any question you want to. If you feel shy, use the problem box. (A problem box is a special colourfully decorated box. Children are encouraged to write their problems down, put them in the box and then the leaders facilitate group discussion to find effective solutions to each of the problems.)

o      If you need a time-out, you can quietly leave the room and come back when you're ready. If you are disruptive, a leader may request you take a time-out until you are able to participate in the group cooperatively.

o      Anything you say in the group is confidential. The only time the leader will repeat anything is if they are worried for your safety. Your safety is our priority in this group. So we will do whatever we have to do to make sure you stay safe (e.g., talking to child welfare authorities or your mother).

o      Everyone helps clean up after snack time.

o      Everyone can play with the toys and everyone must help put them away before the group starts.

**What are the themes in the group?**

Three underlying themes run throughout the group program. They are:

o      self-identity and self-esteem issues.

o      identification and expression of feelings.

o    clarification and challenging of values and beliefs.

**What are the most common topics covered in the group?**

The topics chosen are tailored to meet the needs of the children in each individual group. They include:

o    Understanding wife assault.

o    Sexual assault of children.

o    Alcohol and drug abuse.

o    Anger control.

o    Self-blame.

o    Safety and survival issues.

o    Coping with separation/divorce.

o    Sex-role stereotypes.

o    Non-violent problem-solving alternatives.

o    Assertiveness training.

**Session I**

Topic

Introduction and getting to know each other

Purposes

o    to introduce the topic of the program.

o    to establish the ground rules and to set the atmosphere for the group.

o    to help the children become comfortable and to get to know each other.

Process/Content

Leaders must welcome the children and begin to establish a sense of safety. The children need to know that this group is a special place for children to talk about their feelings and their problems. This is the time to establish the common bond between all the children (i.e., "We're all here for the same reason"). They need to be reassured that their stories will be believed and they will be respected. This is a time to go over the ground rules. Personal disclosure by the group leaders is not necessary here, as it is in the parents' group. Children need only to feel a sense of safety in the group and a sense of trust in the leaders. Confidentiality must be explained.

### Resources/Activities

**TV reporter:**  This is an ice-breaker game that helps children to get to know know each other.  The children pair up with one another and pretend to be reporters.  They ask each other for personal information on four questions, each taking turns.  Then they rejoin the group, introducing their new buddy to the whole circle.  The questions can be selected by the group members or by the leaders.

Examples are:

What is your name?  How old are you?

What is your favourite animal?  Sport?  Past-time?

Why do you think you are in this group?

What do you think will help make this a fun group?

**Session II**

### Topic:

Learning about violence.

### Purposes

o      to provide the children with accurate information about violence.

o      to introduce new rules about violence.

o      to help the child learn non-violent ways of expressing anger.

### Process/Content

Start with a check-in.  Each child gets to share any reactions, new thoughts or recent developments in their situation since the last session.  The topic is then introduced.  Leaders must prepare a brief synopsis of the topic and then move on to encourage the children's participation.  Simple questions should be used to introduce the topic and stimulate thoughts.  What is violence?  Why does it happen?  How does it stop?  How do people fight in families?  In your own family?  Have children give examples from their own lives.  If this is too threatening, use a game or a film to break the ice.

### The Purpose of Games and Activities

o      as an ice-breaker to get discussion going.

o      to make learning fun.

o      to reduce the threat and fear children may feel about discussing their family openly.

o      active play helps children express their thoughts and feelings.

Introduce new concepts such as:

o   It's okay to feel angry, but it's not okay to hurt someone.

o   No one has a right to beat you.

o   No one deserves to be beaten.

o   Use words, not your hands.

o   Take a break if you need to sort out your feelings.

**NOTE:**   Games and activities should **not** be the focus of the session but rather be the facilitator of the information you want to give the children.  Each game and activity must be geared to the maturity level of the group members.  Sometimes children help explain complicated concepts to each other if some of them have a better understanding.  This use of children as the "experts" not only bolsters their confidence but also encourages group cohesiveness and cooperative problem-solving.

## Resources/Activities

**True Facts Game:**  write facts and myths about violence (in simple language) on pieces of coloured cardboard.  Refer back to pages 21-23.  Place them in a special box and have children take turns reading them out to the group.  The children respond by saying if they are True or False.  The leader uses this opportunity to clarify any erroneous information.

**Definitions Game:**  same as above except put words that require explanation on each card.  For example:  Words such as assault, peace bond, restraining order, shelter, separation, divorce, custody.  In essence, any words the children may be exposed to but may not understand.

**Session III**

## Topic

Identification and expression of feelings.

## Purposes

o   to help the children identify and express their feelings.

o   to normalize their experience.

o   to reduce their feelings of self-blame.

o   to begin the process of problem-solving.

## Process/Content

o   Check-in.

o     Review of previous sessions.

o     Leaders introduce the topic by giving examples of different kinds of feelings -angry, sad, confused, guilty. For example, say, "Everyone has these feelings but sometimes we are afraid to talk about them." The best way to overcome certain feelings, such as fear, is to learn more about it. Have the children give examples of how they feel in certain situations. The leader can use a variety of techniques and activities to elicit feelings and offer steps to successfully resolve those feelings.

## Resources/Activities

Films: The "I'm Feeling. . ." series. A series of short films describing a variety of feelings such as scared, mad, confused, etc.

**Things Are Different Now** - twelve year old Joey responds to his parents' separation with anger. This film is useful to introduce the topic of anger identification and anger control. For example, why is Joey angry? What are some bad ways he handles his anger? What are some good ways he handles his anger? How does he work out his feelings?

**How About Saturday** - Tracy has a nightmare. She blames herself for her parents' problems. This film is useful to introduce the topic of self-blame. For example, was it Tracy's fault? What does she worry about?

**Feeling Grab Bag*** - Decorate a special bag and place coloured cards in the bag with different feelings printed on them. Place only those feelings in the grab bag that you think pertain to the group (e.g., anger, fear, confusion, ambivalence). Go around the circle and have each child read out the feeling on the card. Have the child (with help from the group) describe a time when s/he might have had that feeling. Encourage the group to discuss ways to handle the different feelings.

**Session IV**

## Topic

Safety and survival issues.

## Purposes

o     to help children recognize danger signals.

o     to help children learn ways to protect themselves.

o     to help children recognize their right for safety.

---

*      Adapted from Rhonda Freeman's group program for children of separated and divorced families, Family Service Association of Metropolitan Toronto.

o    to help children break the silence?

## Process/Content

o    Check-in.

o    Review of previous sessions.

o    Leaders introduce the topic by talking generally about children's rights and responsibilities.  For example, all children have a right to shelter, food, safety and nurturing.  Today we're going to talk about one of those rights.  SAFETY.  Then move on to define it.  This session is a good place to include information on sexual assault on children.  Introduce concepts such as:

**It's Your Body** - No one has the right to touch if you don't want them to.

**Trust Your Feelings** - Explain the "uh-oh feeling."  For example, "This is a funny feeling people get when they are not quite sure what is happening to them - a bit like a warning signal."  If you think there is something wrong, you're right.

**It's Always Better To Tell** - Tell someone who believes you.  Don't stop until someone does something.

**It's Not Your Fault** - Don't blame yourself.  It's never your fault.

Also include information on how wife assault can impact on children.  What choices do children have when their fathers assault their mothers?  Give children concrete examples of what they can do (for example, call the police, run to the neighbours), and what they should **not** do (for example, try to step in between their Mom and Dad).

## Resources/Activities

Films:  **Better Safe Than Sorry** (2 parts).  This film depicts a variety of difficult situations children might be exposed to and suggests ways to deal with them.  It is a useful tool to use as a beginning point for the discussion on safety.

Artwork:  Get large sheets of newsprint and coloured markers.  Have the children draw a picture of their home.  Mark all the exits in bright red (doors and windows), draw in the phones and include the neighbour's house.  Then help each child mark out an escape path and a plan of action to follow.

Story-telling:  Rehearse potential crisis situations.  Tell a story about a little girl who wakes up at night because she hears her Mommy screaming.  Her Daddy is not supposed to be there (he's on a restraining order) and he's hurting her Mommy.  What should she do?  Any story such as the above can be used as an introduction to problem-solving.  Role-plays are useful to demonstrate different solutions.

**Session V**

Topic

Children have choices.

Purposes

o    to help children develop flexible sex-roles.

o    to help children identify support people in their lives.

o    to expose children to alternative role models.

o    to help children develop their own choices.

o    to help children develop a positive sense of self.

Process/Content

o    Check-in.

o    Review of previous session.

o    Leaders introduce the idea that children have the freedom to make choices in their lives about what they want to be.  Not everyone is the same. Each child is special.  The underlying theme is the harmful effects of sex-role stereotyping and how it limits our choices.  Have the children identify important people in their lives and what they like about them.  Have the children describe what is special and unique about themselves.

Resources/Activities

Films:  **Free to Be You, Free To Be Me** - this film is rather long but parts of it can be used to challenge sex-role stereotypes about what it means to be a boy and to be a girl.  This film facilitates useful discussion about harmful myths. For example, boys who cry are sissies.  Girls are weak and passive.

**Get Used To Me** - a young girl struggles with her feelings of embarrassment because her father is a garbage collector.  This film introduces the idea that "who we are" is more important than "what we do."  It also helps children learn to accept and believe in themselves.

Story-telling:  Read one of the well-known fairy tales, for example **Cinderella** or **Snow White,** and have the children make up their own ending.  Read a modern version of a fairy tale, such as **Paperbag Princess.**  Have the children articulate the differences in each of the stories.

Drama:    **Scenes From A Marriage**

Give the children a typical example of a problem married couples have to work out.  For example, Mary and Bob have been married for ten years.  They have two children.  Last night, they. . .

Have the children act out how this problem might get handled in their own house. Then have the children act out how they think they would like to handle the same problem if they were grown-up and married.

Emphasize the importance of shared decision-making and equality between the husband and wife. This exercise helps the children articulate some of their confusion about sex-role stereotypes. For example, men are the boss, women must obey. It also helps them begin to think about the kind of relationships they want for themselves when they grow up.

## Session VI

Topic

Children are the future.

Purposes

o    to help children solidify their learning.

o    to help children evaluate what they've learned.

o    to identify resources for children after the group ends.

Process/Content

o    Check-in.

o    Review of previous sessions.

o    This session should draw together all the important themes in the group program. It is an opportunity for the leaders to review with the children what they've learned and to evaluate their experience. It also is a time to identify support persons in each child's life in the event of a future crisis. If a child is in need or wants further help, this can be discussed. A special celebration to mark closure should be the last part of the group. A small gift (e.g., a poster) should be given to each child as a remembrance.

Resources/Activities

**Questionnaire:** A written evaluation helps each child articulate specifically what they've learned and their feelings about the group.

**Warm Fuzzies/Cold Pricklies Game:** Each child given an example of a Warm Fuzzy that makes them feel good (e.g., you have a nice smile) and a Cold Prickly that makes them feel bad (e.g., you're a rotten kid). Go around the circle and ask each child to say goodbye to the group members by giving each person a Warm Fuzzy.

APPENDIX A   WHY HUSBAND-BEATING IS A RED HERRING*
by Shirley Endicott Small

There are many ways to make light of wife assault.  It can be dismissed with "women ask for it" or "they enjoy it," to cite two common but inaccurate ideas. The newest way of deflecting concern away from women who live in fear, however, is to wave a red herring called "the battered husband syndrome."

Red herrings are not new in the field of family violence.  Mary Van Stolk, the pioneer in research on child abuse in Canada, reports that initially she was often humourously asked, "But what about battered parents?"[1]  No one jokes about child abuse today or waves the red herring of battered parents in front of child care workers.  Those of us working to bring wife assault out of the closet, however, are routinely taunted with "but wives beat their husbands too."  The implication is that the two kinds of situations are similar in degree, numbers and severity and that we are being unfair to men by concentrating on wife-beating.

The "battered husband syndrome" is an American import having its origin in highly questionable research conducted by a trio of U.S. sociologists - Murray Straus, Richard Gelles and Suzanne Steinmetz.  Interviewers asked 903 husbands and 1,183 wives to report on how they "settled their differences."[2]

The questionnaire listed 18 methods the couple might use -- from a calm discussion through swearing, slapping, beating and finally using a knife or gun. Those interviewed were asked how often they had used each method during the past year.  A "wife-beater" or a "husband-beater" was someone who engaged in the five "most serious" violent acts.  The sensational news of the results:  there are slightly more husband-beaters than wife-beaters in the United States.

The definition is the first questionable aspect of the research.  A man who admitted to having "pushed, grabbed, shoved or slapped" his wife was not considered a wife-beater, for these were defined as "mild" forms of violence. Yet we know that a single slap from a strong-armed man can draw blood from a

---

*  Additional copies of this paper are available from Education Wife Assault, 427 Bloor St. West, Toronto, Ontario M5S 1X7.

1  Van Stolk, Mary.  "Beaten Women, Battered Children."  Children Today, May-April 1976.

2  Straus, Murray, Gelles, Richard, and Steinmetz, Suzanne.  Behind Closed Doors: Violence in the American Family.  Anchor, 1980.

mouth and leave a swollen, black eye. A woman I know was shoved so hard against a kitchen cabinet she ended up with a broken nose.

Secondly, the researchers made no attempt to find out about the consequences of these violent acts. This means that a "hit" from a 200-pound, six-foot-two husband was counted as equally violent as a "hit" from his 120-pound, five-foot-four wife, even though the damage inflicted by these two "hits" might have been very different.

Why didn't they ask how many wives or husbands were actually injured? According to Richard Gelles, they had "good reasons. . .from a strict theoretical point of view it was not worth the energy or time to measure."[3] This lack of concern with outcomes is enough to condemn this research but there are three other defects which mask the amount of violence experienced by women in their homes and inflate the number of so-called "husband-beaters."

The researchers did not consider it necessary to determine who initiated the physical violence. As a result we have no way of knowing how many of the "husband-beaters" were, in fact, assaulted women fighting back or hitting out first (and hard) in hopes of preventing yet another beating. Forty-two percent of the physically abused women who sought shelter at Interval House, Toronto, in 1979 said they had "fought back."[4]

Two items of behaviour which are important to women were not counted as being violent at all -- threatening to hit and smashing or kicking some object. A violent husband often punches holes in the wall, kicks in doors, smashes his fist down on the dinner table to show his wife what might happen to her if she gets out of line. Many women who never actually get hit live in constant fear from threats of this sort. The same is not true for men, according to an earlier study conducted by Richard Gelles using in-depth interviews. He found "no incidents of a wife threatening her husband with violence."[5] So a behaviour pattern that only men use to intimidate their wives is omitted from consideration entirely!

The sample group chosen by the researchers is also statistically suspect. Only couples still living together were surveyed. Had the sociologists included sole support mothers in their sample, the proportion of physically abused women would likely have been much higher. For example, Joyce Kert, a counsellor at

---

[3] Gelles, Richard. "The Myth of Battered Husbands." Ms. Magazine, October, 1979.

[4] Interval House. Annual Report. Toronto, 1979, p. 20.

[5] Gelles, Richard. The Violent Home. Sage Publications, 1974, p. 74.

Opportunity for Advancement, a program for women living on government assistance, reports that in one of her discussion groups, nine out of ten women had been victims of wife assault in their former marriages.

Suzanne Steinmetz chose to ignore these limitations of the study and presented a paper at the 1977 American Sociological Association called "The Battered Husband Syndrome." The press has had a hey-day ever since. Richard Gelles was apparently so embarrassed by all this hoopla that he wrote an article for **Ms Magazine** in 1979 called "The Myth of Battered Husbands." Here he candidly admits that focussing only on the number of hits or shoves, without regard for outcomes or context, "keeps people from coming to grips with the real issues of marital violence. . .the real victims are almost certainly going to be the women."[6]

However, even Gelles' confession contains data which is not supported by Canadian statistics. He claims that as many wives kill their husbands as vice versa. This is **not** the case in Canada. According to Peter Chimbos, in 1969 six times as many husbands killed wives as vice versa. In 1973 the ratio was four to one.[7] Our homicide statistics from 1961 to 1974 show that 60% of all female victims were killed in a family context, more than double the proportion of male victims killed in a similar context.[8] The home is simply a more dangerous place for a woman than it is for a man. Furthermore, it seems likely that many, probably most, of the wives who kill their husbands are battered women who kill to end a long history of beatings. Chimbos interviewed 34 spouse murderers in Ontario prisons - 29 men and 5 women. All 5 women had been victims of long-term beatings.[9]

How much of Canadian marital violence is wife assault? John Byles' study of calls for help to the Hamilton police in 1974 showed women to be the victims 95% of the calls.[10] This figure would seem to imply that 5% of the offenders

6     Gelles, Richard. Ms. Magazine, p. 71.

7     Chimbos, Peter. Marital Violence: A Study of Interspousal Homicide. Palo Alto, California: R & E Research Associates, 1978, p. 35.

8     Statistics Canada. Justice Division Statistics. Homicide in Canada: A Statistical Synopsis. Ottawa: 1976.

9     Chimbos, Peter. "Marital Violence: A Study of Husband-Wife Homicide." In K. Ishwaran (ed.) The Canadian Family. Toronto: Holt, Rinehart & Winston, 1976.

10    Byles, John. "Family Violence -- Some Facts and Gaps: A Statistical Overview." In V. D'Oyley (ed.) Domestic Violence: Issues and Dynamics. Toronto: OISE, 1977.

were women. But we don't know, once again, how many of these women were retaliating or taking preventive action against a chronic wife-beater. Thomas Fleming reviewed all the Durham Region police occurrence reports of "domestic disturbances" for 1974. Out of 337 reports relating to marital violence only 11 of the offenders were women.[11]

Some people attempt to explain these statistics by claiming that men are reluctant to admit they are abused by their wives. However, the same research which generated the "battered husband syndrome" does not support his argument. As Gelles points out in the **Ms Magazine** article, the men in the survey talked more freely about being victimized than did the women. He suggests men are "perhaps less humiliated by being hit and more likely to admit it than their wives."[12]

Those of us working to prevent wife assault strongly believe freedom from assault is every person's right, whether wife or husband. However, we also believe that wife assault is the major problem for the following reasons:

1.      Wife assault does more damage than husband assault. It is assaulted women who end up in doctors' offices and hospital emergency rooms.

2.      Wife assault constitutes the largest proportion of family violence, almost 76% as opposed to 1.1% for husband assault, according to a well-respected Scottish study by Rebecca and Russell Dobash.[13]

3.      Western society has legally permitted wife-beating. The expression "rule of thumb" originated in the common-law tradition that men were allowed to chastise their wives physically provided they used a stick no thicker than their thumbs. There has never been an equivalent rule of thumb for women; wives have never had permission to chastise their husbands. The influence of the "rule of thumb" concept can still be seen in the numerous ways in which violent husbands are "taken off the hook." It is probably easier to get away with committing wife assault than any other crime of violence in our society.

4.      The law permits a husband to rape his wife.* (This permission is in the definition of rape in the Criminal Code.) **Homemaker's Magazine** which goes to upper middle class homes across the country recently found that 20% of the 296

---

*       As of January, 1983, in Canada, it is against the law for a man to sexually assault (rape) his wife.

11      Fleming, Thomas. Violent Domestic Assault. M.A. Thesis. University of Toronto, Centre of Criminology, 1975.

12      Gelles, Richard. Ms. Magazine. p. 71.

13      Dobash, Rebecca E. and Dobash, Russell. Violence Against Wives. New York: Free Press, 1979, p. 246.

women who replied to a questionnaire on violence said they had been forced to have sexual intercourse by their husbands.[14]

5.    A wife-beater often hits two victims simultaneously - his wife and her unborn child. Forty percent of the physically abused women at Interval House in 1979 had been beaten while pregnant.[15] Blows on the abdomen of a pregnant woman are common. This double target is not available for husband beaters.

6.    Traditional ideas of marriage encourage husbands to dominate and control their wives, not vice versa. Women, in contrast, are told by friends, family and church to obey, submit and defer to a husband's wishes. Society does not encourage a wife to dominate her husband by force or otherwise. It is the husband who is encouraged to feel he owns his wife, not vice versa.

7.    Many assaulted women find that leaving their marriage does not remove the fear and violence from their lives. Violent husbands often hound and harass their wives for months after a separation has occurred. There is no evidence that wives who hit their husbands do the same. Truly battered husbands are usually infirm or disabled and the physical removal of the victim from the home ends the violence just as removing an abused child from the home ends the parental abuse of that child.

Does the women's movement not care about battered husbands?   It certainly does - but if people think husband-beating is as common as wife-beating, they will continue to think the problem is just one of "troubled marriages" and arguments that get out of hand. They will not see the need for social and political action to remove the "rule of thumb" principle in our society.   We believe when all groups in the community agree to take responsibility for stopping wife-beating, this will automatically assist that very small number of weak and infirm husbands who live in fear.

---

14    Kome, Penny.   "Women's Place."   Homemaker's Magazine, November 1980, p. 136J.

15    Interval House, 1979, p. 20.

## APPENDIX B   ASSAULT: DEFINITIONS AND PENALTIES*

**Assault —Application —Consent —Accused's Belief as to Consent.**

244. (1)   A person commits an assault when

    a)   without the consent of another person, he applies force intentionally to that other person, directly or indirectly;

    b)   he attempts or threatens, by an act or gesture, to apply force to another person, if he has, or causes that other person to believe upon reasonable grounds that he has, present ability to effect his purpose; or

    c)   while openly wearing or carrying a weapon or an imitation thereof, he accosts or impedes another persons or begs.

(2)   This section applies to all forms of assault, including sexual assault, sexual assault with a weapon, threats to a third party or causing bodily harm and aggravated sexual assault.

(3)   For the purposes of this section, no consent is obtained where the complainant submits or does not resist by reason of

    a)   the application of force to the complainant or to a person other than the complainant;

    b)   threats or fear of the application of force to the complainant or to a person other than the complainant;

    c)   fraud; or

    d)   the exercise of authority.

(4)   Where an accused alleges that he believed that the complainant consented to the conduct that is the subject-matter of the charge, a judge, if satisfied that there is sufficient evidence and that, if believed by the jury, the evidence would constitute a defense, shall instruct the jury, when reviewing all the evidence relating to the determination of the honesty of the accused's belief, to consider the presence or absence of reasonable grounds for that belief.

---

\*   The Criminal Code: R-S-C 1970, Chapter C-34.

## ASSAULT

**245.** Everyone who commits an assault is guilty of

a)     an indictable offence and is liable to imprisonment for five years; or

b)     an offence punishable on summary conviction.

**Assault with a Weapon or Causing Bodily Harm** --Definition of "bodily harm."

245.1 (1)     Everyone who, in committing an assault,

      a)     carries, uses or threatens to use a weapon or an imitation thereof,

      or

      b)     causes bodily harm to the complainant,

      is guilty of an indictable offence and is liable to imprisonment for ten years.

(2)     For the purposes of this section and sections 245.3 and 246.2, "bodily harm" means any hurt or injury to the complainant that interferes with his or her health or comfort and that is more than merely transient or trifling in nature.

**Aggravated Assault**

245.3 Everyone who unlawfully causes bodily harm to any person is guilty of an indictable offense and liable for imprisonment for ten years.

## APPENDIX C   SEXUAL ASSAULT - THE NEW LAW*

On January 4th, 1983 new criminal law about assault and sexual offences came into force.  Some offences such as rape and indecent assault are redefined. Others such as assault are restructured.  Victims of sexual offences have new protection in court.

### Why is a New Law Necessary?

The new law updates the criminal law.  It codifies principles accepted in modern society:

o      All persons have a right to control their own bodies.

o      Men and women have a right to equal treatment.

o      Sexual offences are assaults and should be treated as any other crime.

o      Victims of sexual offences should not be harassed in court.

Before the new law, the crime of rape could not occur between spouses. A man could not be raped.  A woman could not commit rape.  This reflected old views about the role of women, and the position of men.  The new sexual assault offences give the same protection to all persons.

Before, a rape victim who testified in court found herself "put on trial." Old legal rules made proof of sexual offences difficult.  Often the victim's conduct and character were the focus of the trial.  The new law restricts the types of questions the victim can be asked.  The rules of proof now apply to sexual offences as to other crimes.

### What is Assault?

Sexual offences are now a form of assault.  To understand the new sexual assault laws, you must understand how the law treats assault.  The legal meaning of assault remains the same; any intentional use of force against another person, without his or her consent, is an assault.  Touching, slapping, kicking, pushing are all examples of assault if done against the will of the victim.  Any attempt or threat to use force is also an assault.

---

\*      Brochure produced by Communications and Public Affairs, Department of Justice, Canada.

### What if the Victim Consented?

If the victim agrees to the use of force, there is no assault. If the victim agrees, however, because force is used or threatened, either against the victim or another person (i.e. a child), there is no consent. Also, there is no consent if it is obtained by fraud, or by influence of a person in authority over the victim (i.e., a guardian or a school teacher).

The new law recognizes that an accused may have honestly believed that the victim did consent. If the evidence in court shows the belief was honest, and the jury finds that the belief was reasonable, the accused will not be convicted.

### Does "Common Assault" Still Exist?

The new law abolishes the term "common assault." It creates three levels of assault. The first level is simple assault, involving only the use or threat of force. A minor assault may proceed in a summary fashion. The maximum penalty could be six months in jail. If the prosecutor chooses to treat the matter more severely, the court procedure will be more complex. The maximum penalty could then be five years imprisonment.

### What if the Victim is Injured by an Assault?

There are two assault offences which could occur.

1.   If the victim suffers any bodily harm, the penalty could be up to ten years imprisonment. The new law defines bodily harm as any hurt to the health or comfort of the victim that is not petty of fleeting in nature.

2.   If the accused wounds, maims or disfigures the victim, this is a more serious offence. It is called "aggravated assault," and the penalty could be up to fourteen years imprisonment. If the accused puts the victim's life in danger, even without injury, this is also an "aggravated assault."

### Does the Use of A Weapon Make Any difference?

Any use or threat to use a weapon, real or imitation, while committing an assault makes the offence more serious. The penalty could be ten years in jail.

### What is Sexual Assault?

The new law abolishes the old offences of "rape," "attempted rape," "indecent assault female," "indecent assault male." The new offence of sexual assault replaces these.

The new law does not specifically define the term sexual assault. It is, however, any form of sexual assault involving some form of sexual activity. Kissing, fondling, or sexual intercourse with another without his or her consent is sexual assault. The judge or jury decides whether, in a particular case, there was a sexual assault.

A simple sexual assault is the first level of the new sexual offences. Like simple assault, it can be dealt with in a summary way or by a more complex process. The maximum penalty in the first case is six months in jail. If the prosecution treats the matter more seriously, the penalty could be up to ten years in jail. The procedure and the penalty depend on how severe the sexual assault was.

### What if the Victim is Injured in a Sexual Assault?

Again, there are two new offences. If bodily harm occurs, the penalty is up to fourteen years. If the accused wounds, maims or disfigures the victim, this is an "aggravated sexual assault." The accused could go to jail for life. Again, if the life of the victim is put in danger, even without injury, this is an "aggravated sexual assault."

### Are There Other Circumstances That Affect Sexual Offense Charges?

The level of sexual assault charges that imposes a maximum of ten years in jail, applies if the accused:

o     carries a weapon, real or not;

o     uses a weapon;

o     threatens to use a weapon;

o     threatens to cause bodily harm to a third person i.e. child or a friend; or

o     participates in the offence with other people.

### Are There Other Sexual Offenses?

The new law has brought some offences (i.e. rape, indecent assault) under sexual assault. It has abolished some obsolete offences. Many of the old offences remain though. These include intercourse with a female under 14 years, intercourse with a female 14-16 years, incest, buggery, bestiality and gross indecency. Other offences (i.e. pimping) now apply to both sexes. Also, prostitute now means a male or female.

**What Changes Have Occurred in the Prosecution of These Offences?**

The new law makes it easier to prosecute sexual offences. It also reduces the burden on the victim who testifies in court.

**What About Corroboration?**

Formerly, no conviction for rape, incest or gross indecency could occur unless there was evidence to confirm the victim's story. This meant that someone or something else had to show that the offence occurred, and that it was connected to the accused. The new law does away with this need for corroboration. An accused can be convicted of sexual assault, incest, or gross indecency in the same manner as any other crime.

**What Does "Recent Complaint" Mean?**

The old law expected victims of sexual offences to complain about what happened as soon as possible. If there was a complaint, it was used in court to support the truthfulness of the victim. If there was no complaint, the judge or jury sometimes held it against the victim. The new law abolishes the "recent complaint" rules.

**What About Spouses?**

The new law provides that a husband or wife may be charged with a sexual offence committed against his or her spouse. The prosecution can require spouses to testify against each other about all sexual offences. Spouses can also be made to testify in cases of assault or other physical abuse against a victim under 14 years of age. This means that child abusers will not escape prosecution for lack of an available witness.

**What Protections Exist for the Victim Who Testifies?**

New rules about evidence ease the victim's fears that he or she will be "on trial." The sexual reputation of the victim cannot be discussed in court. Discussion of the victim's sexual activity with anyone but the accused is strictly limited.

The accused must give notice of such evidence. The judge must then hold a private hearing (without the jury or the public). The purpose of the hearing is to find out if the accused wants to use the evidence properly. The only proper purposes relate to:

1.     where the prosecution has already raised the issue of the victim's sexual activity.

2.     the identity of someone other than the accused at the time of the offence; or

3.     sexual activity of the victim on the same occasion, that could have led the accused to believe she consented.

The victim cannot be required to testify at this private hearing.

In cases of incest, gross indecency or sexual assault, the judge must tell the victim of his or her right to request a non-publication order. If the victim asks for this order, the judge must make it. This means that the identity of the victim cannot be published or broadcast in the media.

**Where Can I Get More Information?**

Ask a lawyer, call a legal aid office or your local public legal education and information program about Bill C-127, the new sexual offences law. More details are also available from: Public Affairs, Department of Justice, Justice Building, Ottawa, Canada, K1A 0H8, Telephone: (613) 995-2569.

## APPENDIX D   THE HISTORICAL CONTEXT*

All the great religious works -- the Old and New Testaments, the Koran and the Talmud -- give men permission to control women.  As secular laws developed, they incorporated the religious views that men were superior to women.  A husband's right to physically control and punish his wife was a socially acceptable extension of his legal control over her.

In Medieval times, in the Western World, husbands were **expected** to physically chastise their wives. It was their duty.  A widely circulated marriage manual of the 15th century said:

> When you see your wife commit an offense, don't rush
> at her with insults and violent blows . . . Scold her
> sharply, bully and terrify her.  And if this still doesn't
> work, . . . take up a stick and beat her soundly, for it is
> better to punish the body and correct the soul than to
> damage the soul and spare the body . . . Then readily
> beat her not in rage but out of charity and concern for
> her soul, so that the beating will rebound to your merit
> and her good.

You have heard of the expression "rule of thumb."  Its origin was the English common tradition, summarized by William Blackstone in 1767 as the ancient right that permits a husband "to chastise his wife with a whip or rattan (stick) no bigger than his thumb."  Blackstone stressed the need to confine the violence to within "reasonable grounds."  So the "rule of thumb" was away of regulating the husband's right to chastise his wife.

In 1871, Alabama and Massachusetts repudiated the tradition of legal wife beating.  In spelling out what actions by husbands were no longer allowed, the legal language exposed what had been the fate of wives under American and British law:

> And the privilege, ancient though it be, to beat her with
> a stick, to pull her hair, choke her, spit in her face, or
> kick her about the floor, or to inflict upon like
> indignities, is not now acknowledged by our law.

In Canada prior to the 1968 Divorce Act, physical cruelty was not grounds for divorce.  An assaulted wife could claim alimony for cruelty but she had to prove that it was extreme and excessive and involved conduct causing danger to

---

\*   A sample speech written by Shirley Endicott Small for <u>Education Wife Assault.</u>

life, limb or health, bodily or mentally. As an Ontario justice commented in
1920:

> a husband may subject his wife, daily and even hourly,
> to such treatment as makes her life a veritable hell on
> earth and she is without remedy if she is robust enough
> to suffer it all without impairment of her physical
> health or her mentality.

From 1901 to 1965, there was a special offence of wife-beating in the
Criminal Code, which, in fact, was another Rule of Thumb kind of law. A man
could go to jail for two years for beating his wife but only if he caused her
"actual bodily harm." The ordinary legal definition of assault is "the intentional
application of force to another by act or gesture." So that special offence was
a way of regulating wife-beating. Wife assault was legal provided it did not go
too far.

Until the women's movement brought the issue of wife assault to public
attention in the early 1970s by forming Transition and Interval Houses, women
who sued for divorce on grounds of physical cruelty often met the same Rule of
Thumb response from the courts. The 1968 Divorce Act stated that cruelty had
to "render intolerable the continued co-habitation of the spouses" and the
violence could not be condoned by the women petitioning for divorce. Most
wives who petition on the basis of physical cruelty list repeated acts of cruelty
that took place over a long period of time while they were co-habitating with
their husbands. Many judges found this alone amounted to "condonation" and so
turned down the petition.

In one case (Mayberry vs Mayberry) the husband had been convicted of
assault causing bodily harm on his wife, who had then required extensive
hospitalization. Further acts of violence by the husband were cited and
accepted in evidence. Nevertheless, the judge stated that the cruelty was not
of a kind so as to render intolerable the continued co-habitation of spouses but
rather a sort of "tit for tat irritation inflicted on each spouse by the other."

The way to end the Rule of Thumb principle in our society is for wife
assault to be recognized as a **crime** against society. Police officers and judges
should regard domestic violence as just as serious as violence between
strangers. At the moment, wife-beating is still considered a woman's private
dilemma and Canadian society does not take the initiative to protect an
assaulted wife. This principle of non-interference, of assuming that a man's
home is his castle and what he does there is his private business, is the
contemporary form of the Rule of Thumb.

## APPENDIX E   EXAMPLES OF PROTECTIVE ACTIONS

What can an assaulted woman do to protect herself?*

o      Consult a legal expert or family court worker about your rights.

o      Consider laying a charge of assault even while staying at home, or else leave home temporarily until the court case is heard.

o      Find a supportive women's group.

o      Find a supportive counsellor.

o      Become involved in community activities so you are not so isolated and so you can gain self-confidence.

o      Try to predict the times he might blow up and send the kids to a neighbour's or to a relative's house for help.

o      Be familiar with the resources in your community (e.g., local shelter).

o      Try to save a little emergency money for yourself.  Open a bank account in your own name, preferably at a different bank from that of your husband. Request the bank not to send the statements to your home; pick them up in person.

o      Even $10.00 set aside in a safe place will get you a cab in an emergency.

o      Ask your neighbours to call the police if they hear a fight.

o      Plan an emergency exit.  Hide extra clothes, money and/or car keys at a friend's house.

o      Try to involve yourself and your husband with family and friends who do not use violence in their arguments.

o      Take a part-time job outside the home.

o      Upgrade your education or skills with part-time or correspondence courses.

o      Never make a threat or give an ultimatum to your partner, unless you are prepared to act on it.

---

*      Adopted from Shirley Endicott Small and Carol Greenlee, <u>Wife Abuse Understanding The Issues:  A Workshop Manual For Community Groups</u>. Available from Education Wife Assault, Toronto: 1985.

## APPENDIX F   LIST OF USEFUL RESOURCES

The following organizations provide valuable, updated information on both wife assault and other forms of family violence.  You may find it helpful to be on their mailing lists wherever possible.  They include:

**Education Wife Assault**

427 Bloor Street West, Toronto, Ontario, M5S 1X7

Coordinator:  Leslie Lawlor (416) 968-3422

**Centre for Women Policy Studies**

Suite 508, 2000 P Street NW, Washington, D.C.  20036-5997

Phone (202) 872-1770

Re:  Newsletter and quarterly Journal --Response: To The Victimization of Women and Children.

**Family Violence Program**

Ministry of Community and Social Services

6th Floor, Hepburn Block, Queen's Park, Toronto, Ontario, M7A 1E9

Project Manager:  Vicki Bales        Phone (416) 963-2648

**Family Violence Initiatives Section**

Ontario Women's Directorate, 4th Floor, Mowat Block, 900 Bay Street, Toronto, Ontario, M7A 1C2

Provincial Coordinator:  Shirley Mancino        Phone: (416) 965-8260

**Metropolitan Chairman's Special Committee on Child Abuse**

2nd Floor, 443 Mount Pleasant Road, Toronto, Ontario, M4S 1L8

Coordinator:  Lorna Grant        Phone: (416) 440-0888

Re:  literature and resources on child sexual abuse

**National Clearinghouse on Family Violence**

Social Services, Development of Grants Division, Health and Welfare Canada, Ottawa, Ontario, K1A 1B5

Coordinator:  Susan Gilman        Phone:  (613) 995-1050

Re:  Newsletter Vis-A-Vis

**Ontario Association of Interval and Transition Houses**

Room 202, 229 College Street, Toronto, Ontario, M5T 1R4

Coordinator: Trudy Don (416) 977-6619

**Ontario Centre For The Prevention of Child Abuse**

Suite 2106, 700 Bay Street, Toronto, Ontario, M7A 1E9

Director: Sam Morreale     Phone: (416) 965-1900

Re: Newsletter

## APPENDIX G   RESPONSIBILITIES OF AN ADVOCATE

**What Should I Know About the Law?**

You should have a general understanding of the law as it affects assaulted women.

Know the difference between:

o     the Criminal Justice system and the Civil Justice system.

o     criminal remedies and civil remedies.

o     a private charge and a police-laid charge.

Understand the meaning of:

o     legal definition of assault, categories of assault and consequences of the assault charge (e.g., sentencing procedures).

o     restraining order.

o     peace bond.

o     ex-parte order.

o     exclusive possession of the matrimonial home.

o     spousal support versus child support.

o     Family Court versus Criminal Court.

o     Family Law Reform Act (i.e., property settlements).

o     Children's Law Reform Act (i.e., custody and access).

o     Federal Divorce Act (i.e., grounds for divorce, support).

Know the function/role of the:

o     Justice of the Peace.

o     Duty Counsel.

o     Crown Attorney.

o     Police.

o     Legal Aid system.

o     Community Legal Clinics.

**NOTE:**     Request a sensitive lawyer to give your staff group an educational session on the legal rights and options available to assaulted women.

**How do I assess sympathetic referral sources?**

It is your responsibility to have a list of sympathetic resources for your clients (e.g., doctors, lawyers, psychiatrists, psychologists, social workers.) One way to discover their sensitivity on the issue is to meet with them to discuss the possibility of a mutual referral network. Some of the questions to consider asking are:

What is their understanding of why women get assaulted?

What is their understanding of why men are violent?

Are they open to learning more about the issues?

Are they willing to sensitize themselves to the unique needs of this client group?

Are they open for referral of new clients?

Do they have waiting lists? Find out practical information, such as fees, office set-up and availability.

Are they comfortable hearing evaluation feedback from you and your clients?

Are there particular people that they work better with than others?

In addition to their responses, consider your own comfort level during the meeting with the potential resource persons. Trust your own gut reactions. If you feel uncomfortable asking questions or uncomfortable with the answers you receive, it's likely your clients will feel uncomfortable as well. Continue looking! If there is a local shelter in your community, they may well have started a list of useful resource and be willing to share them with you. If time does **not** permit you to meet with a referring agent, advise the client of that and encourage her to let you know what her opinions/experiences are. Many of my resources come from my clients' feedback -- the way they were treated, the worker's sensitivity to them, the worker's ability to offer effective help. (e.g., "I'm giving you the names of two doctors I haven't had the opportunity to personally meet yet. They practice in your area. I would appreciate your feedback after you meet with them. If for whatever reason you feel doubtful or uncomfortable about their treatment of you, trust your guts! That person may not be for you. Call me and we'll find someone else together.") In essence, teach the client her rights and responsibilities to be a confident consumer of service. (Note - do **not** expect this of her when in a state of crisis. That is not the time to be overwhelmed with new demands.)

## EVALUATION

Please comment on the following. This information will be used to evaluate the usefulness of this training manual, and to establish the need for further training material.

1.  Do you deal with wife assault victims and/or their families as a regular part of your work?

    _____

    In what capacity?          _____

2.  Did you find this manual easy to understand?

    _____

    Comments:

    _____

    _____

    _____

    _____

    _____

3.  What did you find most helpful about this manual?

    _____

    _____

    _____

    _____

    _____

4.  What did you find least helpful about this manual?

_____

_____

_____

_____

_____

_____

5.  Do you have suggestions for further training materials of this nature? Please be specific about topics and questions that you would like addressed.

_____

_____

_____

_____

_____

_____

6.  Has this manual influenced you to make any changes in your work?

_____

If so, briefly outline.

_____

_____

_____

_____

_____

7.  Were you comfortable with the value base underlying the philosophy of the manual?

    _____

    Comment.

    _____

    _____

    _____

    _____

    _____

    _____

8.  Further comments/suggestions/criticisms are welcome.

    _____

    _____

    _____

    _____

    _____

    _____

Thank you for your comments. Your concern for assaulted women and their families and the time you have taken to complete this evaluation are both appreciated.

Please return to:

Deborah Sinclair
c/o Education Wife Assault
427 Bloor Street West
Toronto, Ontario
M5S 1X7